RELIVE THE MOST HILARIOUS MOVIE MOMENTS YOU'VE EVER LAUGHED THROUGH—AND MEET THE MASTER WHO MADE YOUR PLEASURE POSSIBLE AND UNFORGETTABLE

Here recreated in delightful detail are the ultimate high points in movie cartoon history—those fantastically funny fireworks of outrageous invention and perfect execution that made every Tex Avery cartoon so very extra-special.

Here brought together for the first time between the covers of a book are memories of Tex Avery himself, and revelations of the processes by which he and his helpers came up with the ideas and the techniques to raise the level of laughter to the theater rooftops.

Here is a book to read in the same way that it was written—with laughter and with love.

TEX AVERY: KING OF CARTOONS

by Joe Adamson

A DA CAPO PAPERBACK

Library of Congress Cataloging in Publication Data

Adamson, Joe.
  Tex Avery, king of cartoons.

  (A Da Capo paperback)
  Reprint. Originally published: New York: Popular
Library, 1975. (Big apple film series)
  Filmography: p.
  Bibliography: p.
  1. Avery, Tex, 1908–   —Criticism and interpre-
tation. I. Title.
[NC1766.U52A922 1985]   791.43′0233′0924   85-11673
ISBN 0-306-80248-1 (pbk.)

Photograph credits and acknowledgments: Private collection of Tex Avery;
Bob Clampett Collection; Metro-Goldwyn-Mayer; Warner Brothers; United
Artists; Tim Walker; Mark Kausler; Walt Disney Productions; Walter Lantz
Productions; Universal Pictures.

Published by Da Capo Press, Inc.
A Subsidiary of Plenum Publishing Corporation
233 Spring Street, New York, N.Y. 10013

All Rights Reserved

Manufactured in the United States of America

TABLE OF CONTENTS

"There is no reality except the one contained within us. That is why so many people live such an unreal life. They take the images outside them for reality and never allow the world within to assert itself."

—Herman Hesse in DEMIAN

"He was disappointed in the world, so he built one of his own. An absolute monarchy."

—Jed Leland in CITIZEN KANE

Acknowledgments

Authors are forever saying, "This book would have been impossible without the following people," although it is perfectly clear that if all those people were never born, the book would still have been written, but the "Acknowledgments" would have said that the book would have been impossible without a whole list of other people. However, the people who were most responsible for this book's being prepared in its present version are the following: Mark Kausler, Tim Walker, David Shepard, Ian Cameron, Tim Cawkwell, Bob Gitt, Mike Barrier, Richard Simonton, J. K. Morrow, Pat Sheehan of the Library of Congress, Roger Mayer of MGM, Erwin Ezzes and Eve Baer of United Artists, Rae Lindquist, Mike Barlow, Phyllis Lipka, David Colker, Barry Snyder, John O'Connor, Friz Freleng and Walter Lantz. Mention should also be made of Lindsay "P." Doran, who researched many of the salient details in the Filmography and typed every single word of the manuscript, some of them three or four times, and only a few of them wrong. This book is dedicated to Lindsay Doran, by the way, and there's no modesty on my part when I say she deserves better.

Portions of Chapter V appeared under its present title, "You Couldn't Get Chaplin in a Milk Bottle," in TAKE ONE, vol. 2 no. 9, December 19, 1970. I fully intend one of these days to get around to asking Peter Lebensold, the editor of that fine publication, for permission to reprint this material. (Incidentally, this article was translated by Max Tessier for the French publication *Ecran* 73, Janvier No. 11, under the title "Rencontres avec Tex Avery.")

1. OF MICE AND CATS

Side Streets

Animation, as a subject, is far more interesting than Millard Fillmore, but historically it's been given the same treatment. When a man goes about writing an inclusive history of film, throwing out cartoons seems to be the first order of business, right after rolling up the sleeves and clearing the desk of rubber bands.

It all began with Lewis Jacobs, who, in 1939, gave Walt Disney credit for being some kind of an artist (something, at least, beyond the aesthetic level of a door-to-door salesman) and then made the statement with a frog in his throat: "Though active only in the sphere of the animated cartoon, he nevertheless is more significant as a film artist than any of his contemporaries," said Mr. Jacobs in *The Rise of the American Film*. Why "though"? Whence "only"?? Wherefore "nevertheless"???

And on it's gone since then, the obligatory passage early in the book explaining that, gee, with all there was to do we just *couldn't* spend any time on animated cartoons, and they should really have a book of their own someday in the sweet bye-and-bye, but meanwhile we'll expend a lot of verbiage on the documentary film, as if that somehow *were* in the mainstream of film history. And so the "book of their own" remains a fantasy, apologetic promontories go on gracing mountains of aesthetic discrimination, Robert Flaherty and Pare Lorentz become icons, and Tex Avery remains a shadow.

Animators spend years drawing circles and drawing forth joy, but the historians are preoccupied with drawing lines. Film is too limitless an art to allow these artificial borders to stand indefinitely, of course, but as long as they do, the same cartoons that used to run ahead of the feature picture are furlongs behind in the Critical Evaluation Sweepstakes. Not only that, but their appreciation is subject to the same condescension toward Popular Culture that once plagued their feature-length cousins.

First, of course, comes the You-Can't-Beat-the-Star-System Stage. The days when John Wayne was the Celebrity and John Ford the Obscurity belong to the distant past, but responsible adults who delight in the adventures of Bugs Bunny, Daffy Duck, and the Roadrunner, put blank looks on their faces when you mention Tex Avery, Friz Freleng, or Chuck Jones—though they have probably read those names off screen credits more often than Otto Preminger's or John Huston's.

When something actually does get into print about the subject, then the Pin-the-Tail-on-Aunt-Emily Effect usually comes into prominence: historians stabbing about in the dark, making any statement that sounds factual, and secure in the knowledge that few of their readers are equipped to prove them wrong. This once allowed people like Lewis Jacobs to scramble Griffith films and Chaplin titles with an abandon that a post-Sarris reader can only find hilarious, but to writers on Animation the *faux pas* is still *de rigueur*. In the presumably authoritative *International Encyclopedia of Film,* Roger Manvell typifies the style when he writes of "the traditional Tom & Jerry series of Tex Avery, the Cat and Mouse characters originated in the late 1940's." Even begging the grammatical question that wants to call Tex Avery a Cat and Mouse, there are almost more mistakes in this sentence than there are words: we find Mr. Manvell crediting Avery with the *creation* of characters he in fact never used even once (nearly all the Tom and Jerrys were directed by Bill Hanna and Joe Barbera, who created the characters under Rudy Ising) and allowing their birth to *follow* their fifth Oscar (they were the star characters of the mid-forties and first appeared in a 1939 cartoon called PUSS GETS THE BOOT). He might as well have been talking about the "traditional" Myrna Loy Westerns of Alfred Hitchcock.

Things go on in this way for several years before writers are willing to take the matter to the advanced stage called the Sociological Sidestep, whereby the films can be seriously discussed and with a certain attempt at accuracy, but only through a point of view that seeks to diminish the individual filmmaker to the level of a pawn in the grip of massive social undercurrents, commercial trends, and class struggles. These people will find musicals of the early thirties interesting only for the light they may shed on the "manners and mores of the times," and they will flock to wartime propaganda atrocities to watch "attitudes" being "reflected"—they speak constantly, in fact, of films as "mirrors," without seeing the wonderland that resides just inside them. In the realm of cartoons we have a stab as blind as Richard Schickel's in *The Disney Version:* Bugs Bunny is not the product of anyone's imagination, he is the personification of The Free World's resistance to Hitler; Mickey Mouse is not a screen personality, he is the very embodiment of the innocence and charm of Rural Americana. To *this* people perk up their ears. They pay attention and money. Simon & Schuster publishes the book, and people go around saying, "Richard Schickel wrote a book about Walt Disney." But he didn't.

A popular subdivision of the Sociological Sidestep is the Propaganda Poop-Out: critics with an ax to grind and a nose for nothing but grindstones. Here we find the moralizing attitude that would champion HIGH NOON and THE OX-BOW INCIDENT while ignoring RIO BRAVO and THE SEARCHERS. In Ralph Stephenson's book *The Animated Film* (known among those familiar with it as "The Outrage of Ralph Stephenson" or, among the more familiar, "The

Outrage of Ralph"), Hollywood animation is written off as pure mindless violence while miasmas of praise are spun for European classics like George Dunning's THE APPLE: ". . . a William Tell complex . . . hints at secret vices . . . it is a mad, suggestive film." Well, THE APPLE isn't so bad, as cartoons of this type go. Observation, detail, creativity, visual excitement, and genuine humor are at a minimum, of course, but the pay-off is amusing and nice enough to nearly justify the time it takes to sit through the film. But one-liners like this are a frightfully limited way for an art form to spend its time; stories and characters with lifeblood in their veins are commodities harder to come by. (*All* of Avery's films are mad and suggestive, if that's what the critic is out for, and what they hint at goes way beyond vice or versa.)

Stephenson's book (also known as "An Ounce of Pretension") is characteristic of another frame of mind, which might be called the I-May-Not-Know-What-I-Like-But-I-Know-Art Syndrome. By this rationale, nothing performed in a given art form can be considered worthy until it closely resembles the entrenched techniques of some other art form. The feature film has long been out of the dark age in which essayists felt they had to call INTOLERANCE "the only film fugue" before getting around to saying something nice about it, and in which THE CABINET OF DR. CALIGARI, because it used expressionistic paintings for backgrounds, was considered the solitary artistic venture of the flickering image. But it's clear that animation is still back there when Ralph Stephenson can say of FANTASIA, "A section to Stravinsky's *Rite of Spring* should be mentioned, because it was favorably received by the composer as a legitimate interpretation of his music." As if that was within hailing distance of a criterion! The Zagreb school of animation, with its Cubist features and its featureless cubes, joins UPA (United Productions of America, creators of Mr. Magoo and Gerald McBoing Boing) in enjoying the kind of recognition that smells of dank museum corridors, while screen cartoonists with inventiveness and originality (whom the Zagreb animators would *love* to emulate, but simply haven't got the budgets) have become the black sheep of the fold.

Where feature film devotees meet, these narrow-minded attitudes have been banished to the remotest outposts of civilization, such as film appreciation classes in Idaho. But where animation, the new underdog of the arts, is concerned, the blinders are still on.

You can see it happening. Some asthmatic college professor looking for attention one day decides that perhaps, yes, animation *can* be considered an art form. But *only* (the disciplinarian in him coming out) if it adheres to certain principles. And what does he pick for his principles? Personal expression, a living contact with people and their culture, a dynamic use of the medium's resources, a range of feelings that cannot be expressed in any other art form, the mystical impulse which turns the commonplace into art? No. It will be a decaying old precept left over from some other art form, and probably some other century. The golden mean, or unity of place and time. Well, there are a lot of us who think animation can be considered an art form, but we don't go to Stravinsky for our guidelines.

"BUGS BUNNY"

Animation, like film, is an art of images: moving, profound, hyperbolic, or just funny, they are images that hopefully express something about their creators' insides, about the conflict inherent in the story, or about life on this particular planet. As images, they have no more obligation to resemble impressionist or cubist art than do the images in the great films to resemble Doré etchings or experimental theater. The ancestors of the animated cartoon include all the visual arts, as well as the drama, the short story, and of course the movies, but it exists independently of these and at its best draws no more from them than inspiration. True, Hollywood rarely used the medium for anything other than to get a laugh (although proponents of UPA's TELL-TALE HEART forget that Harman and Ising made a chillingly effective anti-war film called PEACE ON EARTH that owed nothing to anybody's short story), but the gift of laughter never proved a handicap to Chaplin, Keaton, Fields, or Preston Sturges, and it didn't seem to get in the way of Avery, Jones, Freleng, or Clampett either.

What can animation do that ordinary film can't do, besides get a dog to talk? Walt Disney said a lot when he said, "How does a human being react to stimulus? He's lost the sense of play he once had and he inhibits physical expression. He is the victim of a civilization whose ideal is the unbotherable, poker-faced man and the attractive, unruffled woman. They call it poise."

By its very flamboyance, every aspect of the action in a good animated scene shows up those real-life movies for the earthbound doldrums they really are. An animated character seems unwilling to go from the corner of the room to the door without enduring dramatic transformations of form and texture, undergoing insidious insurrections in all known joints, losing and regaining a generous portion of his clothes, and assuming every split second a new posture more appropriate to some victim of a hard-boiled fit of the ague. He never just *walks* over, unless the guy at the drawing board has abandoned him. In the carefully analyzed action you will find in a good Disney picture, the levels of subtlety and exaggeration, of exuberance and grace, of action and reaction, of reality and fantasy, merge so harmoniously into a hymn to movement that repeated study in slow motion reveals endless marvels.

But all of this, the intricacies and accuracies and hyperboles of a cartoon figure's movement, means nothing without the spark of characterization that brings the movies to life. This is what separates a real animator from the day-to-day cartoonist: like some twentieth-century centaur, an animator must be half draftsman and half actor.

Bugs Bunny is a case in point. *Bugs Bunny does not exist!* (Virginia notwithstanding.) And if he is going to *appear* to exist, and engage in conflicts, and maintain an ascending and descending scale of emotions, and become a box-office attraction and a Hollywood legend, and be referred to in the third person, as "he," it is going to take the concerted efforts of a lot of talented people to turn him from a concept into a creation.

No, Bugs Bunny does not exist. But *he lives*.

Gertie and her Children

The odyssey of the animation art, for all its obscurity, is a fascinating voyage, past Scylla and Charybdis, through underworlds, around lotus eaters—a journey with all the dramatic potential to inspire somebody to make a really bad movie out of it someday. After the early experimenters fiddled around, after Emile Reynaud, Wallace Carlson, J. Stuart Blackton, Emile Cohl, and several others who may or may not actually be called animators according to some definition or another, the first real giant entered this fledgling arena. It is a matter of more than mild historical interest that the D. W. Griffith, the Thomas Ince, the Edwin S. Porter and the Maurice Tourneur of the art of animation were all one person, and did he have his hands full! Winsor McCay was a newspaper cartoonist whose elaborate, detailed drawing style was in no way suited to the sharp, clear lines demanded by conventional animation. However, as there was no conventional animation at the time, McCay didn't let this bother him. When he came out with the five-minute GERTIE THE DINOSAUR in 1914, he created the first major animated cartoon. It had one major drawback, however, in that it made no sense without its creator there to explain it. This rather hampered its success as a box office attraction in the nickelodeons. When played in its intended form as a vaudeville act, however, with Gertie seemingly responding to every remark of her trainer McCay ("Never mind the elephant, Gertie." Gertie hurls the elephant into the lake. "That wasn't nice, Gertie."), it was a smash.

The precocity of this ambitious enterprise, in all its ramifications, is stupefying. It took 10,000 drawings to make Gertie go through her act. (And this was before the bright idea of drawing the characters on transparent cels, to be laid over permanent backgrounds, so McCay was laboriously tracing the same background on every one of his drawings.) Making 10,000 elaborate drawings sounds like an impossible task, but not nearly so impossible as it actually is! I wish I had a nickel for every film teacher who has told me he wished he had a nickel for every student who came up to him all dewy-eyed and said, "I want to make an animated film. Oh, I know it's hard work, but I want to do it. I'll stay up late at night." The poor student inevitably wilts before his time is half up and before his first scene is completed, the point at which the total

16

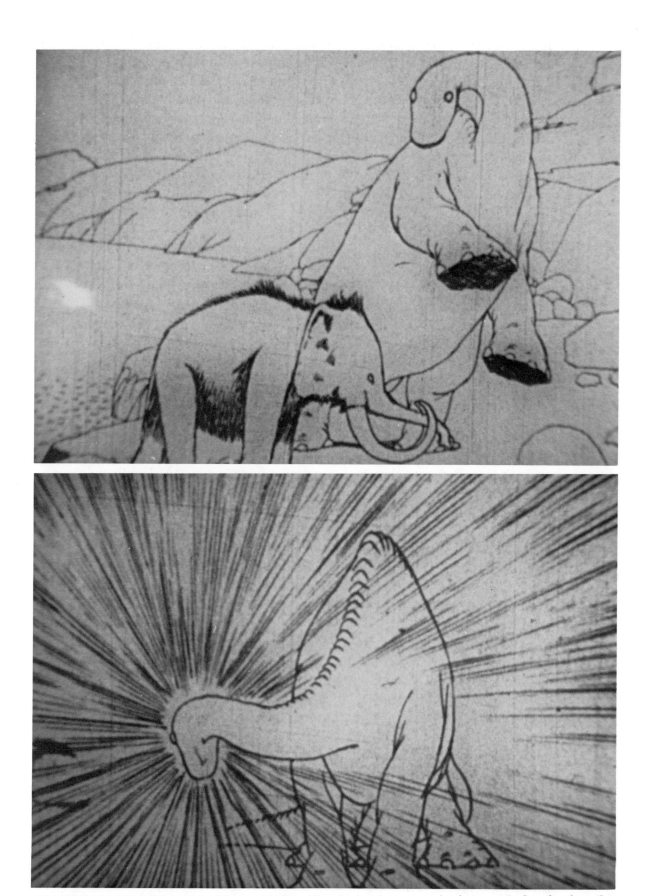

GERTIE THE DINOSAUR by Winsor McCay. The elephant's revenge for being picked up by the tail and hurled bodily into the water is to spray Gertie full in the face with a generous portion of the lake.

impracticality of going any further, the overwhelming impossibility of the entire enterprise, and the general insanity of animation, in toto, defeats him, and he takes the easy way out and makes a documentary.

McCay's achievement was both momentous and monumental, and his lumbering dinosaur first stunned, then mobilized an entire generation of animators, making Gertie the most successful reptilian proselytizer in any known art form. The fascination of moving drawings held hundreds of men spellbound enough to risk starvation, and most of them spellbound enough to endure it. Winsor McCay was the undisputed king of animation for twenty years, but he ruled over a troubled and plague-ridden kingdom.

From 1910 till the breaking of the soundtrack barrier, one cartoon studio after another poked its way out of its inceptive egg, flapped and fluttered its hesitant wings, made one mighty swoop through the air, and buried its beak in the gravel forever. Animation started out, with GERTIE THE DINOSAUR, as a sideshow attraction, and for twenty years worked its way steadily downward.

The pioneer animators were a hardy troupe, but most of them had McCay's dedication without his talent, and McCay's masochism without the entrepreneurial finesse to bring it off. Cartoons were made, one after another, on skimpy budgets, and were never able to command much of a devoted following. They might have attracted a wider audience if they had been somewhat more handsomely produced, but their budgets couldn't be raised until they had attracted a wider audience. The financiers of these operations were caught in a bind in which they were the victims of catch-as-catch-can distribution practices, hostile theater owners, and, finally, audiences who weren't particularly amused. Producers were lucky to receive for their films what it had cost to make them. Distributors, stuck with these things, gave them away with the features. Theater owners, with the cartoons plopped in their lap, often didn't bother to run them. Audiences, having to sit through them, moaned audibly.

And to glance at the cartoons of the teens and twenties is to explain everything. They were turned out weekly by a jolly team of animators who drew what they pleased based on a tenuous version of a "plot outline" (i.e., Mutt and Jeff are painters this week). An onslaught of silly gags would follow, cleansed of all timing, pacing, or any form of comic logic. Each animator simply made everything up as he went along as if doodling his own comic strip, and then at the end of the week all the drawings were collected and photographed frame by frame, according to exposure instructions scribbled in the corner of the page. When the film was finished, it was considered very funny by the men who had spent the last week drawing it. And by no one else. Out would go these reels of film, to play to theater patrons who usually responded by being annoyed or confused. In this way, the early cartoons were among the first films whose chief object in life was to amuse their creators—a very expensive form of recreation later to be rivaled by home movies and the underground.

Animated cartoons became primarily a medium to suit comic-strip characters who wanted to overextend themselves. They were a rich man's comic strip in the same way that feature pictures were a poor man's theater. The silver screen opened its arms to established characters like Maggie and Jiggs, Krazy Kat, Happy Hooligan, the Toonerville Trolley Folks, Jerry on the Job, and the Katzenjammer Kids. Mutt and Jeff, like Sarah Bernhardt, achieved their immortality. Krazy Kat hit the screen with the slogan "Envy me, Mice, I'm going into pictures," but the mice signed contracts with Paul Terry and seemed to envy nobody. William Randolph Hearst financed an entire animation studio and ran it at a loss, just for the publicity value he could give his syndicated comic strips. (If you intended to lose money on your cartoon studio, you were home free.)

From those animated characters not derived from the weekday funnies, the true cartoon began to evolve. Felix the Cat made some scant money for his creator, Pat Sullivan, but only by making Felix the Cat dolls and handkerchiefs marketable, and then only in Great Britain. Paul Terry got started early and established a recurrent character in Farmer Alfalfa, though this guy never turned out to be much more than a straight man for a lot of mice (if one can imagine a more degrading occupation). The Fleischer brothers, Max and Dave, scored a considerable success with Koko the Clown and the "Out of the Inkwell" idea as early as 1915, and by the late 1920s were regularly disbursing dazzling displays of their medium's ever-expanding capacity for extorting wonderment. Interestingly enough, Koko the Clown was probably the only cartoon character in the history of the medium who really did exist.

Through an odd device called the Rotoscope, the Fleischers were able to make their animation more lifelike, and at the same time combine cartoon characters with live action figures within the frame. It was chiefly the act of bringing things slightly down to earth that earned them their success (and, paradoxically, made their films cheaper to produce). The Rotoscope combined a film projector with a drawing board, making it possible to film an action with real people, then trace it, frame for frame, with pen and ink. Koko the Clown was simply a cartoon rendition of Dave Fleischer in a clown suit. Then, when the projector-plus-drawing board apparatus was combined with a camera, it was no problem to combine the cartoon drawings with a live-action accompaniment that was rephotographed under the drawings. For the entire duration of the long-running "Out of the Inkwell" series, the older brother Max played the real-life cartoonist, while the younger brother Dave played his cartoon character. Audiences were at least able to make a granule of sense out of this arrangement.

The Rotoscope outlived the inkwell and the clown. Eventually it was discovered that you could photograph a person prancing about in some peculiar fashion and magically transform him into any old thing. The movement of the dancing ghouls in the "Night on Bald Mountain" sequence of FANTASIA is Rotoscoped movement, but it was human men who acted out the required gyrations, while animators, Circe-like,

Key drawings from LITTLE RED WALKING HOOD, a Tex Avery cartoon of 1937, indicate the animator's job in establishing only the extremes of movement.

made them into monsters. Professional dancers provided the original footage for the "Dance of the Hours" segment, probably doing their best to forget that animators were going to spend months turning them into ostriches and hippopotami. The Rotoscope became a prime tool for reinforcing the tenuous bridge between reality and a world of sheer imagination.

Another technique that blossomed in the rocky soil of the twenties was the use of the in-betweener. It was practicality that hastened his existence, and his task was a mighty lowly one, but he helped advance the art toward its most creative stages. It is simple fact that in an animated movement of twelve drawings, it is only the key drawings—say, drawings one, six and twelve—that determine the character and the nature of the movement. All the others are mostly filler. The animator does only the key drawings, and then turns them over to his underpaid flunky assistant to complete the action. This developed, in the more sophisticated animation studios of subsequent decades, into an imposing hierarchy of animators, assistant animators, in-betweeners, breakdown men, and cleanup men, and even—for those who went whole hog, like Disney—a separation between character animators and effects animators (to do splashes and wisps of smoke). Though the final result seems to be the reduction of the animator to one solitary post on an assembly line, the intended and usually effected outcome was to allow the creative aspect of animation to be separated from the mountainous drudgery.

Even in these days of film societies and film archives, animation of the silent era is rarely in evidence. Perhaps it's just as well. The deficiencies of silent cartoons are weighty and depressing compared to the fancy flights of Walt Disney in the first decade of sound.

Walt Disney did his first animating in the Midwest in a ratty advertising outfit called the Kansas City Film Ad Company, which was also the starting point for his brother, Roy Disney; his musician, Carl Stalling; his first key animator, Ub Iwerks; the first directors of Warner Brothers cartoons, Hugh Harman and Rudy Ising; and the eventual nexus of the Warner organization, Friz Freleng. Among others. (There may be some reason why so many of the major names of animation emerged from this wholly forgettable flea-pit organization. Or it may be, like any resemblance to actual persons living or dead, purely a coincidence.)

When Disney scored a smash with STEAMBOAT WILLIE, the first sound cartoon, it was against the shrewd business judgment of those who knew better. But the combination of sound and animation had already proved itself irresistible at every transitory appearance it had gotten a chance to make. McCay's GERTIE presentation had achieved this effect. A Mutt and Jeff entry entitled SOUND YOUR A caused a mild sensation with a conversation between Mutt, Jeff and the drummer in the orchestra in which the drummer got up and spoke and Mutt answered back in balloons. And when the first of the Bouncing Ball cartoons hit the screen in 1925, uniting moving images with the trilling of the audience, it got everybody so riled up that they wouldn't sit still for the feature till they'd had a chance to go back and sing along again. (Years of ridicule and an unsuccessful attempt at revival have obscured the original popularity of the Fleischers' Bouncing Ball series of the twenties.) The addition of sound turned animation into something more than moving drawing. It now had a measure of magic heretofore denied to it. A new outpost of reality was established.

Disney capitalized on color as well as sound. He was not the first to make color cartoons, but he quickly secured the exclusive animation rights to Technicolor's three-color process, and suddenly his Silly Symphonies looked remarkably better than anybody else's color cartoons. Disney was privy to all the colors in God's original spectrum, while anybody else in the business was stuck with orange and green, and variations thereof (light orange, dark green).

But Disney's accomplishments were more than technical. He was the first in the nascent, uncertain art form to wage an all-out confrontation with the study of motion. His analysis of the real principles of momentum and inertia, and his stylized adaptation of them to the realm of animation, elevated the movement in his films to previously unknown heights, and made it an element worth watching for its own sake.

And, hand in hand with movement, came its Bobsey twin, the problem of characterization. Disney was the first to face the problem of moving each character in a way distinct enough to set him apart from any other character. When he made his own version of THE TORTOISE AND THE HARE it abounded not in stale, convenient jokes about running, but in comic routines derived from the contrasting personalities of the two main characters. Perplexingly, the cartoon characters in the silent days were all puppets. The characters in Disney's Silly Symphonies had the breath of life imparted to them.

The whole animation industry, in fact, had new life after the advent of Disney's innovations. The animators who worked under him were suffused with an enthusiasm for their work and a sense of pride in their craft they had never known before. The established firms that had to compete with him were forced into an imitation of his care and perfectionism. Disney kept his company running through the spare years of the Depression and managed to accomplish what devoted cartoon studios had always tried for and never achieved. He reinvested all income to improve his films, rather than going home with a profit in his pocket. He gained control of his own distribution to foil the pirates and the profiteers.

There were other cartoon studios in the thirties. Harman and Ising aped the Silly Symphonies with Looney Tunes and Merrie Melodies for Warner Brothers, then switched over to Happy Harmonies at MGM (everybody apparently being firmly convinced that you weren't a real Disney imitator until you'd copied the idea for his series title). Krazy Kat survived at Columbia for some time into the decade, though by this time he was neither Krazy nor Kat. The Fleischer brothers bought the rights to a comic-strip character named Popeye and enjoyed a fair amount of success. (And if anyone can think of a less promising idea for

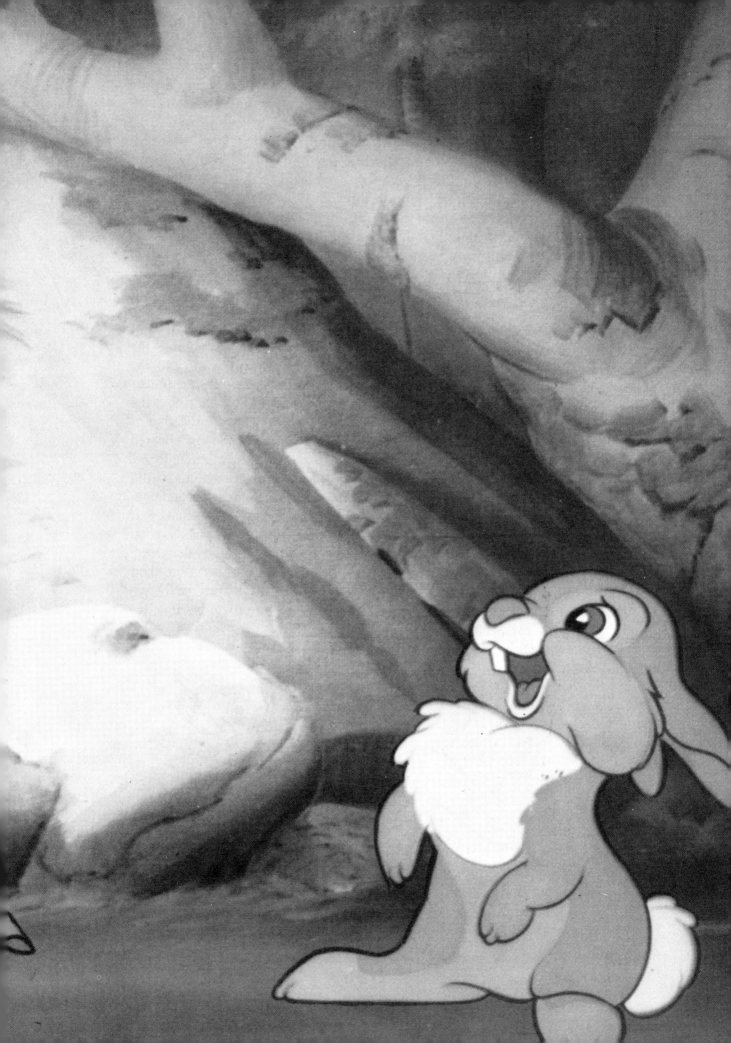

a cartoon character than a wizened old one-eyed sailor, I should like to hear about it.) But for an entire decade Disney eclipsed all other activity in the medium, and by the early forties was presumptuous enough to have several features in production at one time.

The cuteness for which Disney is often taken to task sits, like Griffith's Victorian sentimentality, at the basis of an overwhelming imagination, a precision sense of craft, a dynamic personality, and a film-making genius. When the emotion is genuine and talent is at its peak, as in BAMBI and FANTASIA, the result is absolutely brilliant. When neither of these conditions hold, as in PETER PAN and CINDER-ELLA, the result, as critics today are fond of reminding us, is appalling. Since the 1950s, Disney's name has been inseparably wedded to a treacly concept called "family entertainment," and that curse is not very easy to shake.

Increasingly, animation at the Disney Studio became a matter in which craftsmanship replaced the artistry and excellence replaced the excitement. With the financial setbacks induced by the war, and the move to a sterile new studio in Burbank, an atmosphere of resentment consumed the love and devotion that had once been rampant, and the organization wound its inevitable way from an isolated congregation of devotees into a pretty ordinary bureaucracy. Many of the most talented people left, and Disney's competitors found new sources of strength.

Animators he had spent tons of money to train went on and did their best work for somebody else. There was now a managerial and popular acceptance that made the production of cartoons a less chancy, if never a surefire, venture. A pattern was set in which good comedy, good animation and clever visual effects were expected and usually delivered. Eventually, Hanna and Barbera set the scene for doomsday with their television-aimed computer animation (HUCKLEBERRY HOUND was the first, in 1959). Great cartoons with care put into them became history, like everything else with care put into it. But for twenty years before that Disney's short-subject rivals ran riot in the trails he had blazed.

Pluto Pup, complete with "breath of life."

26

Methods and Madness

Many's the time that a friend or acquaintance has come up to me and said, "But, Joe! What does a cartoon director *do?* Does he say, 'All right, Bugs, let's take it again from the top'? Ha ha ha ha ha." I try to associate as little as possible with these people.

The truth is that the men who made the drawings and the men who wrote the stories were all taking orders from a single guiding intelligence who was, in effect, the sole creator of these films to a greater extent than can be said of the directors of any other branch of filmmaking.

The action in an animated cartoon is so completely under the director's control that it becomes a medium in which the filmmaker's imagination not only *can* run absolutely riot, but genuinely *has* to, if his films are going to rise to the expectations of the art. The cartoon director is granted a level of freedom that extends in all directions in every dimension in every frame—his territory ranges from fixing the dramatic conflict to determining how the trees are going to look. But, like any freedom, the freedom of the animation medium brings with it its own responsibility. The stylization, the exaggeration, the free-wheeling disregard for earthly reality, are all liberating enough for a scene or two, but it's a thrill that can wear out pretty quickly, unless it's given a steady guidance beyond the momentary.

The liberation is inherent in the medium; the control is up to the individual director. Most of them, of course, settle for the comfortable rut of the talking cats and mice, and the casual walking on air that comes to a halt when the character realizes the ground is gone. But the better directors don't let unreality get off so easy. Each one of them, when he puts his mind to the task, manages to come up with a separate set of physical laws and behavioral properties that constitute his own world. Chuck Jones' Coyote can fall five miles from a precipice and still be alive when he gets to the bottom. Tex Avery's Wolf could probably endure such a fall, but he is more likely to develop brakes on the way down. It is the creation of the director's own universe, and the maintaining of that universe, that makes animation a medium capable of individual, personal expression, and what allows us to tell one animation director from another, even when some wiseguy has taken the credits off the film.

In a good live-action film, one feels the presence of the director in

27

every frame. In even the most unremarkable animated cartoon of the 1940s and 1950s, the director has dictated the contents of every frame on a complicated chart, supervised the preparation of each, and completely re-vamped any that didn't meet his approval. In a *good* cartoon, the action is so meticulously worked out that the levels of expression are infinite.

The methods by which the director achieved this control had mostly been developed since the days of the silent cartoon—the days when there usually was no director, and no guiding intelligence. They derived chiefly from the practical fact that all elements of an animated cartoon must be mapped out to a fraction of a second before anyone even considers the notion of putting film in the camera. Animation is probably the only known form of movie-making in which the actual employment of movie film can safely be classed as post-production work.

First came the storyboard. The idea of paying separate individuals to do nothing but think up gags and stories and waste endless hours tinkering with structure would have seemed like wastrel foolishness to the pinch-penny practitioners of the pre-Disney sub-subsistence animation economics. And it was of paramount importance that when story planning did become a widespread habit, it took the form of hundreds of drawings, rather than a neatly typewritten script, so that story and gag construction were conceived and worked out with an eye for visual detail that would cover all contingencies. With all the drawings posted on a board, in sequence, it was possible to see the characters and their situations interacting and resolving themselves before any actual animation was done. With the autonomy often granted to directors at the better cartoon studios, they had enough control over their material to wholly reject a finished storyboard, or to totally revise a satisfactory board in accordance with personal notions of the human comedy.

But it was after the storyboard that the healthiest supplies of creativity were demanded. The movement, the character expression, the whole tone of the film was to be determined by the rhythm and frequency of the drawings. And the precise number of drawings, and the length of time and degree of importance granted to each—all of this was determined by the director on a complicated piece of paper called an exposure sheet. In Mickey Mouse's time, it was done in a slightly different format on a bar sheet, and the chart's necessity seemed determined only by the problems of synchronizing action with music, but the essence was generally the same. The director needed some way to line up every note of music, every syllable of uttered verbiage, and every nuance of physical action; to tell the animators, frame for frame, what he wanted them to do. The timing, so crucial to animation and so essential to good comedy, needed to be fully worked out on paper.

But even with this wholesale, programmed, before-the-fact calculation, some room had to be made for error, some way had to be cleared to give the animator a rehearsal space. And this was the function of the pencil test. All the pencil test consisted of was the proper photography, according to the exposure sheet, of the animator's drawings as they came off his drawing board, before being traced onto transparent cels and painted in the proper colors. This gave everybody a chance to see the completed sequence as animation (and not as a series of drawings) before the commitment to full and expensive production was made. In the heyday of theatrical animation, when they were working under tight budgets that today look like money to burn, it was customary to go back and change fifteen to thirty percent of the work after the pencil test had revealed its deficiencies. Again, the problem of hiring a separate man and a separate camera just to photograph pencil drawings all day seems like an expenditure vastly unjustified by this complicated mechanical process. But when quality and fidelity to a personal vision seem worth fighting for, the pencil test serves a necessary purpose for the perfection of smooth animation and successful comedy.

The peculiar thing about it is that every one of the techniques enabling the animation director to assume his place as the artistic center of his film was developed during the thirties at the Walt Disney Studios—the same studio which soon became notorious for never allowing a director to take any control. It was fully impossible to be a director, in the complete, dictatorial sense of the word, at a studio where every move anybody made was supervised and criticized by the man who became a legend. Personal expression was less to Disney's liking than analysis, refinement and purification; and, in the end, he was the guiding intelligence behind everything that came out with his name on it. But it was Disney who paved the way for the brave men who followed, the he-man directors who shouldered the abundance of intricacies, responsibilities and metamorphoses this imposing medium demanded, and tasted of the joys of its flexibility and its range—Chuck Jones, Friz Freleng, Bill Hanna and Joe Barbera, and, of course, His Satanic Majesty, Tex Avery.

2. RED-HOT RIDING HOOD MEETS THE 300-LB. CANARY

Daydreams

No artist, in any century, on any continent, in any medium, has ever succeeded in creating his own universe as thoroughly and overwhelmingly as Tex Avery. The action in his cartoons is not representational action, nor is it the kind of action one expects from an animated cartoon. Avery's films will roll along harmlessly enough, with an interesting situation treated in a more or less funny way. Then, all of a sudden, one of the characters will lose a leg. And hop all over the place trying to find it again. Or one guy will take off the other guy's head and toss it out the window. Or his nose will jump off and run away. Or three characters will sprout where once there was one, and dance all over the frame in a frenzy. In SLAP-HAPPY LION, a kangaroo hops into its own pocket and disappears. In BILLY BOY a goat is rocketed to the moon and eats it. In NORTHWEST HOUNDED POLICE, a fugitive wolf reaches

Six heads to indicate horror in HAPPY-GO-NUTTY (1944).

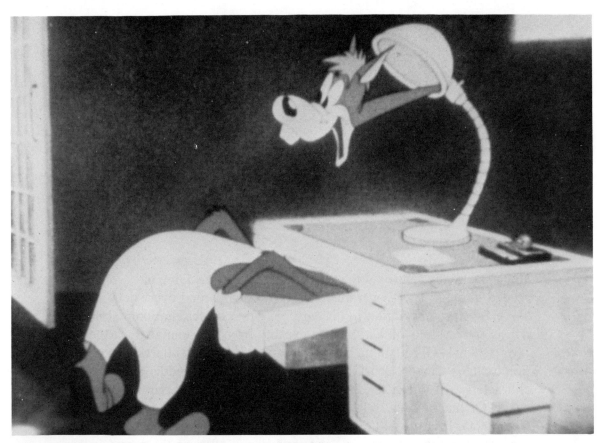

A couple of Avery pretzels: LITTLE RURAL RIDING HOOD (1949).

his hideout in the wilderness, slams eight different doors into the same doorway, then turns around and, without uttering a gasp, drops his jaw to the floor with a thud. In HOMESTEADER DROOPY, a pistol gets wounded in the midst of a gun battle, and its owner must send a bullet through it to put it out of its misery. In SEÑOR DROOPY a matador extends his cape for a charging bull, and the bull charges right into it and out of the third dimension. The matador plainly exhibits both sides of the cape to prove that the bull isn't hiding up his sleeve. Then, from under the cape, he produces a small egg. When he hatches the life-size bull out of the robin-size egg, a roar goes up from the crowd, and the bull is suitably outraged.

There are times when one feels sorry for Avery's characters, for all the beatings, smashings, pulverizings, contortions, inflations and diminutions they are forced to undergo. But eventually one learns to nurture a high regard—even awe—for these beings who brave such punishment as this and live to tell about it.

And they live, there's no doubt about it. They may be chopped in half, beheaded, fragmented, burned to cinders, disemboweled, turned inside out or twisted into pretzels, but they are restored to normalcy within seconds, and maintain a vigorous vitality through it all. After the most horrendous and total demolition they are capable of leaping into action again at four frames' notice.

No other cartoon director has ever asked so much of his characters; but then, no other director has ever allotted them such endless elasticity. Avery's boneless, bloodless creatures seem to consist of some indefinable substance which allows them a physical liberty bordering on license. It is certainly not flesh or fur, but neither is it plastic or putty. Sometimes it bends in highly improbable places. Sometimes, when punctured, it deflates. Sometimes it stretches for miles. Sometimes it can be jammed into a container many times too small for it. Sometimes, when hit too hard, it shatters and must be pasted together again offscreen. What is this miracle material of a thousand lives? We might call it Averex, and perhaps if we keep demanding it at our hardware stores and hobby shops they will put it on the market for us.

Avery's visual style has a multitude of associations, connected as it is with those he influenced as well as those he was influenced by. It appears today as a composite of the oblong blobs of Don Martin, the comic derangement of Virgil Partch and the bloodcurdling viciousness of Gahan Wilson. The violence in Avery's films comes in heavy, baroque doses, but it is an unobjectionable, distracted form of violence that is all joy and no pain. So long as all the bodily parts keep restoring themselves, like Prometheus' liver, there is less a sense of destruction than of exhilaration. Avery has not only the daring and imagination to pull such outrageous gags, but the animation skill, the directorial finesse, the filmic logic and the comic sense to put them over so they are shocking and funny instead of just weird.

And Avery's cartoons are funny. If I have taken this long to get to that point it is because it goes without saying once you have seen a few. Some of them seem a little overdone, some of them are disappoint-

BLITZ WOLF: Nobody does anything in a small way in an Avery cartoon.

ing, some are repetitious, and some are so loud and brassy it's annoying, but they are all funny. Every one contains at least one parcel of comic genius, and often there are so many it's uncanny. Avery can cram more things into seven minutes than most filmmakers get into an hour. His better films are hilarious and the best of the bunch are as funny as anything ever put on the screen. Avery's sense of comedy presides over all the timing, delivery, sound effects, movement, mood, story construction, character development—over every minuscule step of the way from inception to execution, so that everything's funny, even things that have no right to be funny. For instance:

The gag in THE SHOOTING OF DAN McGOO where a man described as having "one foot in the grave" hobbles into the room with an entire plot of ground, an erected tombstone and a decorative tulip all cumbersomely attached to the end of his right leg. (In the next shot, of course, he is not described as having one foot in the grave and the plot of ground is not there.) The hombre sidles up to the bar and calls, "The drinks are on the house!" At which point everybody in the place dashes straight outside, hurries up the fire escape and stands around on the roof having drinks in the snow. The crux of this is not so much the particular gags, which are almost obvious, and sound like something you or I could have come up with at a party, but the brazen vividness of the presentation. With such enthusiasm this moron comes loping, CLUNK! CLUNK! into the bar, dragging this grave on his foot, and for what reason we'll never guess. In accordance with all the standards of good comedy, the laughs are prompted just as much by the character's reaction and attitude as by the action itself. The same goes for the utter joy of the barflies as they dash, to a man, outside for their drinks, and the total silliness of their wanting to stand in the cold snow just to make it worth the first man's while to have said his line.

Or the gag in HOUSE OF TOMORROW, where it is finally revealed to all the world how that light goes off when you shut the refrigerator door. Just as you thought, a little man runs out and shuts it off. Again, this is the kind of gag you might expect your nephew to run up and tell you. And again, the genius of its execution is absolute. It's a little gnome, with a funny hat and a beard that reaches to his toes, who toddles out of a little door (where you must surmise that he lives) and heads for the little lightswitch. He is just taller than a lump of butter but not quite so high as a pint of milk. Perhaps just the size of a good round egg. And he toddles past the groceries and back into his house. All the interesting little sidelights of an everyday absurdity are examined, worked out and paraded on the screen in front of us.

An essential feature of Avery's juggling with the laws of physics is that, like all things in the cinema, it was done before. In the ancestral twenties it was nothing for animated Mutt or animated Jeff to misplace his head and hardly notice. And Felix the Cat's passion for detaching his tail and using it as a baseball bat was matched only by his fondness

Or the one about the fellow who checked the boxing gloves for horseshoes and uncovered a thoroughbred horse:
LONESOME LENNY (1946).

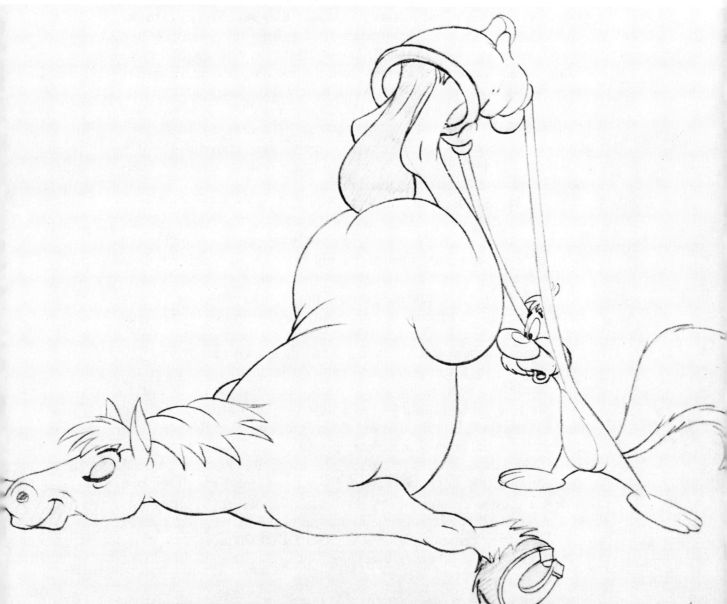

for question marks and exclamation points as convenient props. Avery admits the similarity, but the difference constitutes a world. One is not surprised by such actions when they are carried on by spare little black and white drawings who speak in balloons and whose only audio impact is created by a convivial organist biding his time till the feature starts. One is simply not convinced of their presence. It was Disney who sounded the death knell for such loosely knit panegyrics in the interest of a more convincing set of realities. Once the new realities were established, and color and sound united to make the action convincing, the way was clear for Avery to introduce the absurdities again, this time into a whole new context. He does not abandon the reality of the self-contained cartoon world, he just extends the limits of reality beyond the bounds of credibility. His action is convincing. His cats and dogs prance around inside a definite physical dimension, and when their eyes roll out, or their teeth crumble, or their feet get punctured and shrivel to a shred, there is just no question but that this is really happening up there. Though nothing is right, everything opposes contradiction. He doesn't ask you to believe it, you can't help but believe it.

This is a style that approaches surrealism, but deceptively. It obviously is not reality, but neither is it wholly illogical. Avery's cartoons usually proceed in clear, Aristotelian fashion from first principles that are preposterous. Nor can this be fantasy, since the ruthless, boisterous nature of his humor is a far cry from the piddling sort of *Peter Pan* nonsense we associate with that word. Rarely does Avery address himself to a sea of childish faces. There's never a "let's pretend" or a "make-believe" atmosphere to his cartoons. It's always "This is it!" One cannot label his special brand of reality very conveniently. It is a unique and individual set of factors and circumstances that exists nowhere else on Earth or Venus.

The biggest clue you will find, in fact, to the origin of the state of Tex Avery's humor is the humor of the state of Tex Avery's origin. It was Texas that gave birth to the most widespread and influential form of American folk humor, the tall tale. Look closely at these straight-faced stories of the ranch that was so big they used the state of New Mexico for a grazing pasture, or the man who dug the Rio Grande for himself because he was thirsty, or the bronco who bucked off a saddle so hard it landed in the middle of the week after next. Listen hard to these legends that provide their own parody and you will know where a man gets the nerve to come up with a gag like the one about the stubborn dog out to block up gopher holes as fast as they can be burrowed, until he has a paw over each of them, and still they are being dug, until there are eleven holes all over the yard, and damned if the old dog doesn't come up with eleven paws to cover them all (GARDEN GOPHER). Or the one about the Western badman demonstrating his shooting prowess by blasting one little fly on one little hill on one distant cliff on the horizon—a hill so far away that he can only hear the echo of the insect's scream reverberating through the neighboring canyons (DRAGALONG DROOPY).

Avery has the power of every great humorist, from Aristophanes to Woody Allen, to take a serious matter and keep blowing it up out of all proportion until its gravity begins to shrivel. Chaplin has said it is one of the great godsends to the sanity of the human race that if you exaggerate any hardship far enough it becomes funny. Avery, in his Rabelaisian zest for zaniness, exaggerates just about everything, and far enough to be hilarious. It's not easy to find a moral or a political point of view in films that are made up out of sheer comedic virtuosity. The only slant you will find him giving a subject is the age-old slant of the comic perspective: the idea that once you have been coaxed into laughing yourself silly at a serious concern, you will begin to see the real absurdity in taking it so seriously in the first place.

It is the artist as magician, as visionary, as conjurer of unknown kingdoms, as creator of a new reality that is strongest in Avery: the expressionistic revelation of the inner self that characterizes von Sternberg, Murnau, Fellini and Welles—along with Heller, Joyce, Barthelme and Tolkien. Avery's personal form of madness made filmic adds a new dimension to the terrain of the film medium. Dimension Praecox.

Tunes and Melodies

It took Avery a long time to reach this pinnacle of omnipotence in his own distended universe, but it didn't take him long to make funny cartoons. His first films were made for Warner Brothers in 1935 at Leon Schlesinger's studio, and consisted of Looney Tunes and Merrie Melodies at a time when there was a difference between Looney Tunes and Merrie Melodies. It must be said that the Looney Tunes, made in black and white with a different rationale and starring a primitive version of Porky Pig, gave him greater opportunities to develop a gag style than did the Merrie Melodies, which were mostly second-string imitations of the Silly Symphonies. When one is aware of the Herculean comedy Avery is capable of, it's rather painful to watch the few good gags in the early Merrie Melodies, like I ONLY HAVE EYES FOR YOU, I LOVE TO SINGA and A SUNBONNET BLUE, battling against a storybook world of make-believe that is reminiscent more of something regressive than of something fun. The childish atmosphere of a thing like DON'T LOOK NOW, which asks us to get interested in a rivalry between Dan Cupid and an unbecoming sprite hoping to represent the babyhood of Beelzebub, makes its adult gags (the devil ruining a wedding ceremony by paying two kids to run in and yell, "Stop, Daddy!" right in the middle) look rather peculiar, and the combination only gives cause to stop and wonder which audience Avery thought he was aiming at.

The free and eccentric nature of the Looney Tunes left room for more experimenting. There are some great moments, like the one in PORKY THE RAIN MAKER where one of Porky's barnyard geese waddles up, finds a "cyclone pill" lying on the ground, pecks at it uncomprehending, swallows it and is instantly hurled by his insides to all corners of the frame, at the conclusion of which he is startled enough to speak English and exclaim, "Well! Imagine that!" in a sterling tenor. In MILK AND MONEY the mortgage on the farm is being foreclosed by a Mr. Viper, a villain villainous enough to be identified as The Snake, who slithers his serpentine way back to his carriage, coils around the separate spokes of the wheel, describes an arc into the driver's seat and takes off (a sublime piece of animation by Chuck Jones). Viper is vanquished in the final footage as Porky arrives with

A barely recognizable Porky Pig (before a streamlining process gave him a new image) hanging around in the arms of his father. Frame from MILK AND MONEY (1936).

Closeup of a frog croaking: CROSS-COUNTRY DETOURS (1940).

43

his racetrack winnings in a car that's at least two miles long. (Nobody is anybody in an Avery cartoon until he can drive a car that's two miles long.)

Avery's Warner cartoons are all amusing, but in general they are too tame in tone to engender much enthusiasm. Even when a burst of wild invention appears, like the silenced cuckoo in AIN'T WE GOT FUN who quietly produces a pocket watch which he shows around, it is marred by a slow, deliberate pacing that stretches things out too evenly for any momentum to be gathered. This is partly a result of the economy that had to be observed, whereby every drawing was milked for all the footage it was worth, every position was held for at least two seconds, and any actions that couldn't be repeated till they grew stale and flaked away were better left undone. And you can just bet that all your favorite gags in any one Warner cartoon will be certain to pop up again in the next one. One of Avery's Merrie Melodies is called OF FOX AND HOUNDS, and it is funny enough, but it's not much more than the same gag repeated three times. Three times!

WACKY WILD LIFE (1940).

Also injurious to the overall effect are the double takes these incredulous characters insist on doing to overemphasize all the good gags. The creation of an absurd universe is not quite possible so long as its characters continue to be stunned at every infraction of the rules of physics. Nor is it facilitated by inconsistencies developed inside the insanities. CIRCUS TODAY, for instance, features an act called the Flying Cadenzas, who proceed to flap their arms and fly to their respective trapezes. Once there, a slipup sends a Cadenza hurtling to the sawdust offscreen, leaving his brother to advertise for a replacement. One or

44

Gratuitous insanity in THE PENGUIN PARADE (1938).

An urban streetcar invades the Arctic setting of DANGEROUS DAN McFOO (1939).

For no particular reason, Egghead was a recurring character at this point in time. He is seen here tipping his head in CINDERELLA MEETS FELLA (1938).

the other of these gags is fine. The two of them in conjunction only cancel each other out. This is the sort of trouble a man is just asking for when he refuses to abide by the laws of the universe he was born in.

All that can be said of his Warner cartoons is that the best of them are consistently funny. Avery was soon to pass beyond that. Avery's associates at Warner's recall that he was capable of acting out hilarious activities for his imaginary characters to imitate, but that the humor was easy to lose in the process of animation. Clearly, an approach would have to be uncovered that was suitable both to a prodigious comic mind and an extremely technical art form. But in his brighter flashes of novice inspiration he gave us glimpses of the havoc to come.

THE PENGUIN PARADE, for instance, handles its swing music with a lively spirit, and it seems perfectly appropriate when a pleasant three-part harmony on "When My Dreamboat Comes Home" is abruptly cut off, for the duration of one beat, to allow the trio time to make grotesque faces at the audience. An announcer penguin comes on stage to

Model sheet for PORKY THE WRESTLER (courtesy of Bob Clampett).

47

introduce a song-and-dance number in a magnificent speech that lasts a full minute in single shot, and it takes you nearly half that time to ascertain that he isn't making a fragment of sense, except for an intelligible "Leon Schlesinger" stuck in the midst of the double-talk. In HAMATEUR NIGHT, a conductor stands up before his five-piece band to commence the overture, and suddenly he's a one-man band and they five conductors. The curtain, rather than rising on the first act, just falls down on the stage. In DANGEROUS DAN McFOO (a comic rendition of Robert W. Service's poem, "The Shooting of Dan McGrew") Avery refreshingly provides no rational reason why the first round of a fist fight in a Yukon saloon should prompt a trolley car to storm through the swinging doors and clang its bell. Just as irrationally, the tough guy is not given a rubdown between rounds, but a shave and a haircut.

Technical finesse and a respectful treatment afforded to serious moments set off the comedy in THUGS WITH DIRTY MUGS, a neat parody on the gangster cycle, with quick cuts, interesting camera angles, and a sense of real authority to its series of ridiculous jokes. Killer Diller is shown systematically looting every bank in town, from the First National Bank to the Worst National Bank, in a succession of taut, brisk scenes which appear, montage fashion, to cover several months, until the ominous headline appears on the stands, "87 Banks Robbed Today." Killer is a caricature of Edward G. Robinson, but he can also do an impersonation of Fred Allen, so he stands up and does one. The biggest heist provides the highest tension as the circle of Killer's flashlight closes in on a safe in the dead of night. Killer is not fazed for an instant when the safe turns out to be a radio. He and his henchmen flop to the floor to listen to the "Lone Ranger Show" and are apprehended right in the middle of the Ovaltine commercial.

Technical finesse and the impressive handling of a serious moment also come to the rescue of CROSS COUNTRY DETOURS. (Perhaps the best of a bunch of travelogue and documentary parodies that Avery started with THE ISLE OF PINGO-PONGO in 1938, and followed with A DAY AT THE ZOO, BELIEVE IT OR ELSE, DETOURING AMERICA, WACKY WILD LIFE, CEILING HERO and AVIATION VACATION. These films attempt to be more laughable than the short subjects they are making fun of, and a few of them actually succeed.) A great job of dramatic animation underlines a stalking bobcat, while a narrator bewails the fate of the innocent baby quail about to be his prey. The intense drama shatters when the bobcat suddenly breaks down, pounds the ground with his fist, and admits between sobs that he hasn't got the heart to go through with it.

PORKY THE WRESTLER contains the first fully sustained comedic elaboration of a surreal idea in an Avery cartoon, and seems to mark the first full-blooded unleashing of the Avery spirit into the cartoon world. Porky's opponent in the ring swallows a pipe and begins chugging around like a train; Porky and the referee, trying to stay out of his path, end up following him around like railroad cars, and a succession of train gags follow: the bell is set up in one corner and begins clanging like a crossing signal, the water cooler rocks back and forth on a previously

An animation drawing from PORKY'S DUCK HUNT (1937) (courtesy of Bob Clampett).

All the model sheet there was for PORKY'S DUCK HUNT, done by Tex Avery himself (courtesy of Bob Clampett).

steady floor, and one member of the audience looks out the window, and, seeing scenery go by, realizes he's missed his stop(!) and runs out clutching his suitcase.

Pleasing as many of these are, there are only two Warner films, out of sixty made in six years, that are worthy of the name Tex Avery. One is PORKY'S DUCK HUNT and the other is A WILD HARE. One gave birth to Daffy Duck and the other spawned Bugs Bunny. One set the tone for all Tex Avery and all Warner Brothers cartoons to follow, and the other created the character that toppled Disney from his unassailable throne. Remarkable achievements, but neither Avery, nor the characters, nor the studio stopped there.

PORKY'S DUCK HUNT, looniest of all Looney Tunes, arrived in the middle of 1937, Avery's second year of cartoon-making, and it has all the self-assurance of a grand old master. "Be v-v-very, v-v-very, v-v-very q-q-quiet," Porky tells us, lurking in the lilies. And no sooner does a single stray duck glide into sight than thirty-seven hunters spring up out of the neighboring reeds and fill the air with din and buckshot. And when the smoke clears, onward wings the solitary mallard, unconcerned. It is then up to one sharp-eyed shooter in the next marsh to bring him down. He aims, fires, and straight to the ground comes one small plane, with horrifying, realistic sound effects and a very confused pilot who sits cowering in his downed aircraft. Porky absently pulls a 180-degree switch on the direction of his gun, which allows him to aim skyward, pull the trigger, and sink himself. Then a gang of trout get drunk and do a beautiful rendition of "Moonlight Bay."

With all this going on, it wouldn't seem as if the duck had much of a chance to steal the show. And he doesn't. He isn't drawn with quite the flair you expect him to be, and his voice isn't there yet, either. As a concept for Daffy Duck he's not much more than germinal. About all that really strikes you about the character is his reaction to the deadly fact of his being the object of a hunt. He doesn't care. He thinks it's funny. And his cavalier attitude toward the earnest fellow who is supposed to be hunting him down really *is* funny. This is seven leagues from anything a cartoon character of the thirties was supposed to be, and just the sort of thing Disney would never let one of his directors try. In his best scene, the screwball duck does nothing more than dance away into the distance, in one long, mad shot—no camera movement, no great dialogue, just "Hoo-Hoo, Hoo-Hoo, Hoo-Hoo!" and over he goes, hopping on the water, turning handsprings, bouncing on his head, tumbling in the air, sidling on his heel, splashing on the surface, skidding far out of sight, and then swooping back again for another round. A simple idea, but a fantastic shot, one that owes a lot to some graceful and demented animation by Bob Clampett. Then, after the plain and predictable final gag, and you're just in the act of telling yourself you've seen a pretty funny cartoon, on comes this maniac again, and sails over the production information and the slogan "That's all, folks" that comprise the end title, swinging on the T, spinning on the apostrophe, sliding on the folks, springing to the Warner Brothers, scooting over the Vitaphone, sallying

50

HARE-UM SCAREUM (1939) by Hardaway and Dalton.

ELMER'S CANDID CAMERA (1940) by Chuck Jones.

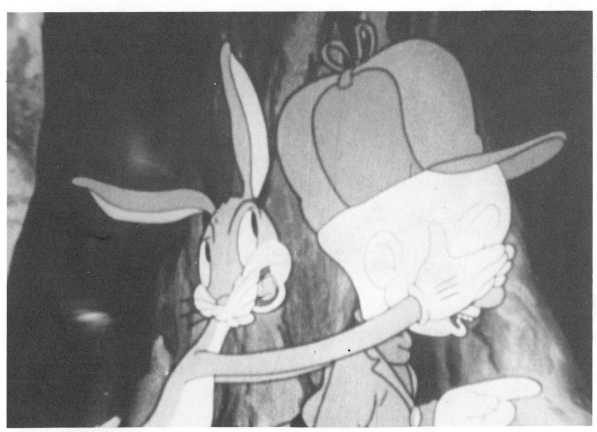

A WILD HARE (1940) by Tex Avery. Elmer Fudd's personality crystallized simultaneously with Bugs'.

A WILD HARE.

around the Studios, steering starboard over Schlesinger, swooping side-ways to the small print, swaying slinkily to the copyright, and then swip-ing, swirling and skipping to the end of his spastic spree, and you know you've had nothing less than a feast.

Bugs and Willoughby the hunting dog fall to their doom in THE HECKLING HARE (1941) a scene animated by Rod Scribner.

You get the same feeling out of A WILD HARE, but in a much calmer way. The breezy insouciance of the main character extends to the character of the whole film. WILD HARE was the fourth in a series of rabbit-hunting pictures, but the first to make such a hit in the theaters that there was cause for alarm, and the one that crystallized Bugs' personality for good (while PORKY'S DUCK HUNT was the first of all the duck cartoons and was instantly successful, though Daffy's personality wasn't fully developed until later). PORKY'S HARE HUNT, 1938, and HARE-UM SCARUM, 1939, starred a fearless rabbit who bolixed up all attempts to murder him, on a design fashioned by Bob Clampett using leftover gags from PORKY'S DUCK HUNT. Both cartoons were directed by Ben Hardaway and Cal Dalton, who managed to misdirect the character so thoroughly that he was more annoying to the audience than he was to his antagonist. (In HARE-UM SCARUM he sings, "I'm so goony, loony tuney, touched in the head/Please pass the ketchup, I think I'll go to bed." Seeing a Looney Tune is cited as the cause for his dementia.) The third of the series was directed by Chuck Jones in 1940 and called ELMER'S CANDID CAMERA, and here the rabbit slowed down and became far less aggressive, though just as annoying. The Woody Woodpecker laugh ("Hee-hee-*hah*-hoo, Hee-hee-*hah*-hoo!"), the Groucho Marx walk, the dopey voice, and the awkward character de-

53

sign all combine to make him look pretty stupid, but Jones' film has a tranquil, offhanded atmosphere that's a distinct relief.

Remarkably enough, A WILD HARE, also 1940, depends, point for point, on the same gags that make up ELMER'S CANDID CAMERA, and, magically, they're all funnier the second time around. This is one cartoon in which the slow, deliberate pace of the Warner Brothers Averys really pays off, and seems to be exactly what the situation demands. There are only three or four gags presented, each one fully developed into a nice little routine, and they all ripen beautifully. In the nicest of them (a gag pulled hundreds of times since, which hundreds of imitations don't succeed in showing up) Bugs has Elmer Fudd convinced that he's shot him, and the throes of his death spasms are so horrifying (screams of "Gettin' dark! Dark!" and frantic cries of "Don't leave me!") that after he twitches to a convulsive conclusion, Fudd is aghast at himself for doing what he intended to do all along, and runs in terror to a tree, collapsing against it, sobbing, "I killed him! I'm a wabbit killer! I killed the cute little bunny wabbit!" Behind him, as he wails on, the cute little bunny wabbit stealthily approaches, cautiously folds back the flap of Fudd's jacket, exposing him, then lets fly with a hefty boot. And just when you're ready for Elmer to fall down, or jam his little red nose in the tree trunk, he sails, grandly, up the entire length of this mighty timber, meets a branch with a resounding gong, and comes smoothly and precipitously to his knees at the rabbit's feet.

Avery directed three more Bugs Bunnies while he was at Schlesinger's: THE HECKLING HARE, TORTOISE BEATS HARE, and ALL THIS AND RABBIT STEW. Each one is marked with the solid, steady, self-assured rhythm of the first, a distinct divergence from the helter-skelter nervousness of the Duck. It took talent and imagination to sustain Bugs' popularity and to make the great Warner Brothers cartoons of the forties and fifties, but a legacy like A WILD HARE and PORKY'S DUCK HUNT was just the head start the studio needed for the impending years of their supremacy. Avery was never again to create a cartoon character with the infinite charm and appeal of Bugs Bunny. But then, neither was anybody else.

Between the Lions

Avery's development from this point on was centered around his own personality, which is even more rich and strenuous, if possessed of less commercial value on cereal boxes. From 1941 to 1954 he ran his own unit at Metro-Goldwyn-Mayer (though all the cartoons claim they are "Made in Hollywood, U.S.A.," the MGM lot was in a dumpy old place called Culver City), where he replaced Hugh Harman and Rudy Ising, and was responsible for practically every MGM cartoon of the forties and fifties that did not star Tom and Jerry. Right from the start he began cooking up his intoxicating hyperboles, assuming outsized liberties, and

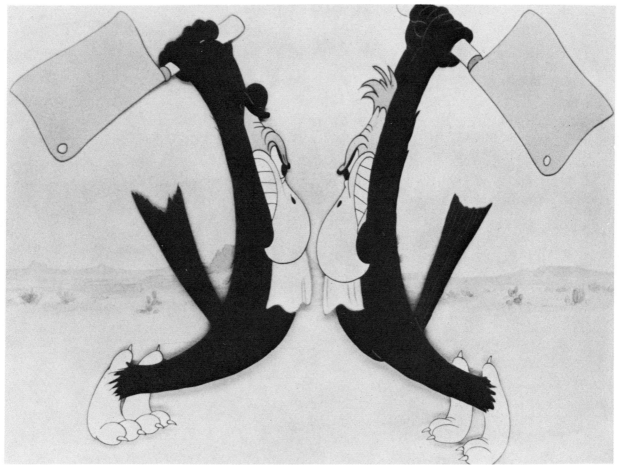

WHAT'S BUZZIN' BUZZARD (1943).

55

THE BLITZ WOLF (1942).

taking his characters shamelessly to pieces, and it's here that the relation between his cartoons and the day-to-day world of theatrical animation began to grow more and more tenuous.

His first film for the new studio, THE EARLY BIRD DOOD IT, looks like it could be one of the better Warner Brothers efforts, with typical Avery gags like peeking under the water in a lake as if it were a rug. But the black humor that had been bubbling under the surface begins to be increasingly in evidence. The story concerns a worm being chased by a bird being chased by a cat. In the end, the bird eats the worm, and the cat eats the bird. Not recommended for children.

WHO KILLED WHO? (1943).

The second MGM cartoon, THE BLITZ WOLF, and the first to be released, is a wholehearted comedy on as unfunny a subject as Hitler. Avery seems to have gone all out on this one, stuffing it chock full of the kind of wild humor, gag upon gag, confusion worse confounded, and savage exaggeration that was later to become routine: a B-19½ that looks like a 747, a militaristic Sergeant Pork, enormous phallic weapons that seem to extend forever, an opening pronouncement claiming, "The auto tires used in this photoplay are fictitious," a Good Humor Tank carrying the slogan, "I don't want to set the world on fire," and an awful lot of noise. Which transmits to us practically no attitude toward Hitler. One-sided propaganda may befit a lesser talent, like George Dunning or Stephen Bosustow, but a demonic nature like Avery's is not so easily confined to simplistic campaigns for the "good."

Then there's BATTY BASEBALL, which races into its footage

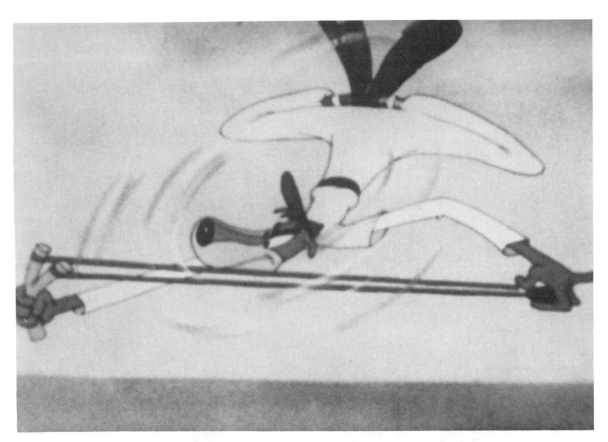

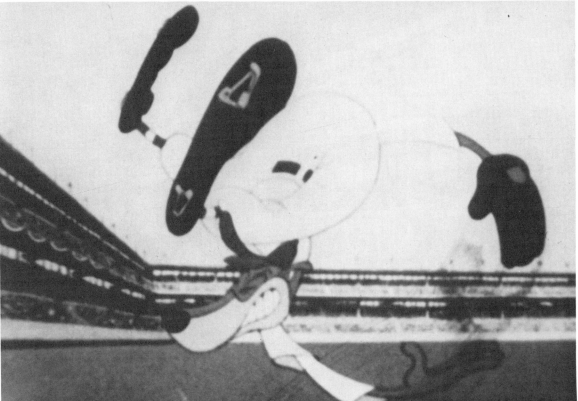

Ed Love is responsible for this dynamic animation from BATTY BASEBALL (1944) though the slingshot gag belongs to Ray Abrams.

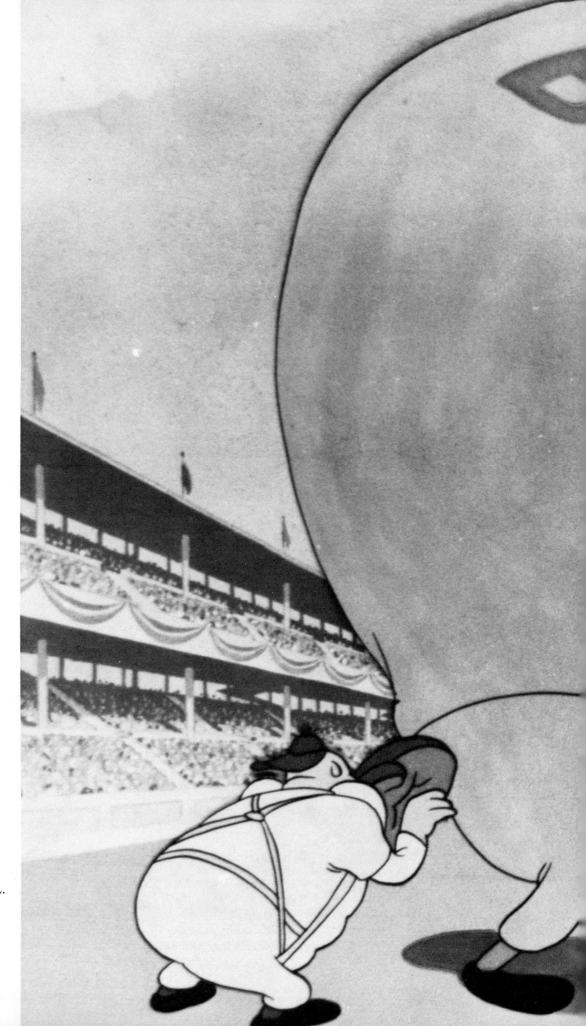

BATTY BASEBALL.

RED
SKELETON

Animation drawing from WHO KILLED WHO?

WHO KILLED WHO? Interrogating some slightly suspicious insiders.

before the credits come on, and suddenly three wonderful gags are crowded into one hysterical minute before an outraged base runner stops everything and complains, "Who's directing this picture? Where's the MGM lion?" And they go back and start over. Things grow tragic as a heckler in the stands goes red in the face screaming, "Kill the umpire!"— and white and then gray when they actually do.

But the gem of this early batch, the fifth of the sixty-six films made at MGM, is WHO KILLED WHO?, a relentless spoof that takes on ghost stories, horror stories, murder mysteries, and all other comers. Characteristic of its macabre lunacy are the two eyes, glaring in the dark, that turn out to be affiliated with no particular organism, and loom ominously out of their doorway, just farther than they should, only to get the door shut on them. The grotesque sight of a door opening to let a corpse drop past the camera and thud to the floor is somewhat qualified by the equally grotesque sight of another corpse directly behind it, and then, after it falls, another one behind that. The graphics and the animation draw forth all the horror possible, and the effect is genuinely ghastly, but by the time seventeen of them in a row have hit the floor it's just crazy. Finally, one of the cadavers pauses, in his drop, long enough to trill the words, "Ah, yes! Quite a bunch of us, isn't it!" And down he goes, followed by seventeen more. At one mad juncture the detective, in his scattered search throughout the house, reaches a door labeled, "Do not open until Christmas." As this seems relevant to nothing, he opens it to reveal a closet containing Santa Claus, waiting around for December. Mr. Claus is visibly disturbed and slams the door, leaving all logical questions unanswered.

All this begins with the victim of the crime, sitting in his study in the middle of a lonely night, reading a book called WHO KILLED WHO—FROM THE CARTOON OF THE SAME NAME. He has a poster board sign on his chair establishing his identity: "The Victim." "At the sound of the gun, the time will be exactly twelve o'clock," intones the skeleton who inhabits the cuckoo clock, and into the room looms a pistol the size of a cannon which chimes the hour. The victim writhes and gesticulates through a great death sequence, hammed up for all possible, and impossible, histrionics, and instantly a detective bursts upon the scene. "Who done it?" he yells into the vacant room. "Everybody stay where you are!"

The locale of all this is a grand, palatial layout, with great marble balustrade stairs, on which a chase takes place involving several Lovecraftian creatures, whose origins and eventual outcomes remain as much a mystery as Santa Claus. "Reach for the ceiling," the detective is told, and the camera tracks back to take in the entire ballroom while the detective obligingly reaches the necessary three stories to get to the ceiling.

The gags here annotated are not anything unlike what could have transpired in a Tex Avery Warner Brothers cartoon. But, in their abundance, in their adroit timing, and in the act of their impenetrable accumulation, a new style is announced.

The detective demands that all weapons be put on the table and winds up with an arsenal in WHO KILLED WHO?

Characters and Characteristics

We now come to that stage in our narrative when Mr. Avery, in an attempt to recapture the success of his discovery of Bugs Bunny, endeavors to create exciting and lovable cartoon stars to gladden the hearts of youngsters all across America and to adorn comic books, soap dishes,

Animation drawing of Screwy Squirrel.

beach balls, party cups, and vitamin pills for years to come. And it would have to be said that Avery's talent was too great to allow him to fall into the "family entertainment" trap he practically aimed himself at. There are directors whose chief medium of expression on the screen is the face of their main character, but Tex Avery isn't one of them. His effects—more distancing than endearing—come off more like Godard's or Eisenstein's than like Disney's. He enjoys telling us it's a cartoon we're watching—*his* cartoon. His feature players comment on the dialogue in progress. In NORTHWEST HOUNDED POLICE one fellow skids clean past the sprocket holes and off the celluloid in his attempt to scurry into a movie theater, where he catches the very picture he's appearing in. Avery treats his characters with such a directorial distance that never once do any of them come across as the justification for having made the film. Most of them, like the detective in WHO KILLED WHO? or the penguins in THE PENGUIN PARADE, are only as interesting as they have to be to have funny things happen to them. They are simply pawns on a fascinating chessboard where Avery is king of both sides and champion player.

In 1944 and 1945 there is a concerted effort to get Screwy Squirrel crammed down our throats in four pictures in a row, SCREWBALL SQUIRREL, HAPPY-GO-NUTTY, BIG HEEL-WATHA, and THE

Screwy Squirrel.

One of Droopy's model sheets: SENOR DROOPY (1949).

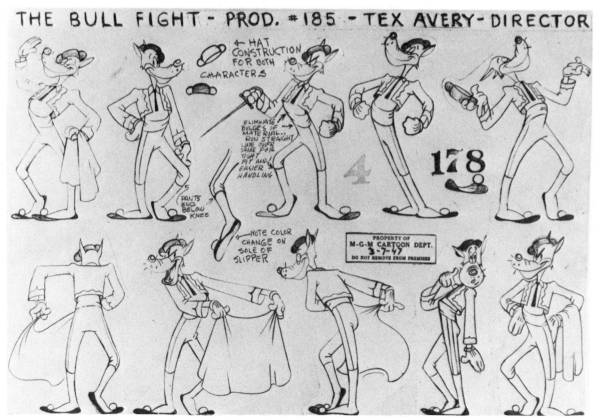

The Bad Guy: Droopy's antagonist from the same film.

SCREWBALL SQUIRREL.

Avery's Droopier sketches.

SCREWY TRUANT, followed with a fifth in 1946, LONESOME LENNY. Screwy Squirrel is Daffy Duck taken one step further than he absolutely has to. A funny character who is slightly insane, like a Harpo Marx or a Woody Allen, has a subversive sort of captivating quality, but a maniac who resolutely flaunts his insanity is little more than frightening. His starring vehicles take a hardy constitution to endure, though they exhibit their creator's comic genius all the same.

In a burst of three quick cartoons, HENPECKED HOBOES of 1946, and RED HOT RANGERS and HOUND HUNTERS of 1947, George and Junior, a cartoon parody of MICE AND MEN, were born and died. George (nasty, brutish, and short) and Junior (brontosauric in size, Cro-Magnon in comprehension level; ever repeating George's sentences in the misguided notion that this will help him to understand them; ever devoted to George and ever spoiling all of George's plans out of an excess of devotion) are bears or dogs or some indefinite organism, and one is never very sure whether one wishes to see them achieve their professed goals or not. Their farewell appearance in HOUND HUNTERS, however, is a decided triumph—for Avery, if no one else. (And their attempted comeback in HALF-PINT PYGMY in 1948 is a decided disaster. Avery seems to have made this film for the sole purpose of proving that George and Junior are bears. So *that's* all settled.)

The most appealing of Avery's MGM characters, and the only one that my readers are likely to remember—mostly because he managed to make it onto the inside covers of the Tom and Jerry comic books—is Droopy Dog. Droopy starts rather early on in Avery's MGM days, and has a career spanning twelve years and sixteen films, ranging all the way from the inadequate and unimaginative DROOPY'S DOUBLE TROUBLE to the incontestable and unimaginable DRAG-A-LONG DROOPY. An imperturbable semicolon surrounded by exclamation points, an emotional stoic in an epicurean universe, an understatement lost in the "valley of exaggeration," Droopy is cute enough, and some of his cartoons are great. But there is just no denying that what you really remember about them is the bad guy encountering a moose head who turns out to have been a whole moose hiding behind the wall, or the bad guy beckoning a tuxedoed waiter out of God-knows-what-corner of a roughhouse saloon to usher Droopy offscreen. The bad guy.

Droopy's first appearance is in Avery's fourth cartoon for MGM, DUMB-HOUNDED, in 1943, where he reworks a gag that wasn't funny in TORTOISE BEATS HARE, an early Bugs Bunny attempt: one fellow reappearing at every turn in the path of his frenzied opponent. The essential difference, of course, is that in the Bugs Bunny picture a lengthy explanation is provided for the continual reappearance, while by this time, only two years later, Avery feels the need for no such encumbrance—just wherever this escaped convict turns, there is Droopy, the police dog, who has gotten there first, and is asking him something like "What kept you?" There is no forgetting the first instance of this in DUMB-HOUNDED, where Droopy, standing at the door of the criminal's apartment, drawls out a precautionary, "You stay here while I go

George and Junior in HALF-PINT PYGMY (1948).

DUMB-HOUNDED (1943).

and call the cops. Now promise me you won't move," while the crook speedily whips down the fire escape, leaps in a cab which takes its curves on all four wheels on the neighboring walls, drives a scooter out of the cab and onto a train which goes from zero to 200 miles an hour in one frame, hops a motorcycle out of the train and onto an ocean liner that runs with its prow up like a motorboat, and drives a jeep out of the ship's hold and into a plane before takeoff, and after landing emerges from the plane on a hardy steed which gets him to a tiny log cabin in the middle of the Northern Canadian woods, which he has no sooner entered than he faces Droopy standing there pointing an accusing finger at him and complaining, "You moved."

This situation, so inevitable it's predictable, soon wears itself out, so that the main center of attraction gets to be the outlandish takes of the convict. A "take," in Avery's definition, involves screaming, yelling, falling apart, hiding behind your eyeballs, making the noise of a locomotive

NORTHWEST HOUNDED POLICE (1946) (seen below and on the next two pages) amplifies the central idea from DUMB-HOUNDED (right). Droopy, like Hope, springs eternal. The Wolf never ceases to be amazed.

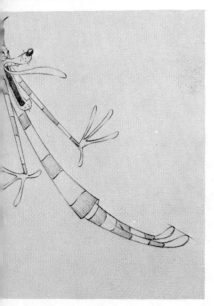

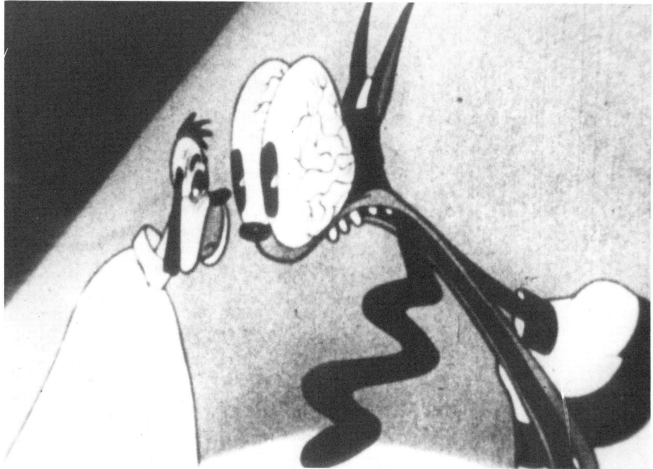

One of Droopy's paroxysmal villains stealing the scene from him in THE SHOOT-ING OF DAN McGOO (1945).

or a Stanley Steamer, turning your tongue into a stairway to your jaw, losing your pants, turning your horizontal stripes into vertical ones, and otherwise going on to prove that you can pass muster as a Tex Avery character.

From 1949 on, Droopy pops up rather often, though his villains still succeed in stealing attention from him with stunning regularity. In DARE-DEVIL DROOPY he's up against a colorful bulldog named Spike (all bulldogs are named Spike) in a competition for a circus job which quickly reduces itself to a series of manic blackouts, Droopy un-wittingly foiling all of Spike's wicked schemes just by being innocent. Spike tries showing up Droopy's dexterity with the 1000-pound barbells by putting stickers over all the zeroes. Droopy then hoists the object as if it were a one-pound toy. When Spike tries it, the stickers peel off, and the full tonnage of the barbell promptly crushes him through the floor of the stage. Droopy is fired out of a cannon and lands pertly in a safety net. Spike is fired out of the same cannon, and flies past the net, through the tent, across the sky, and into the ocean, where he sinks a battleship. Later, Spike falls through a safety net, and expires in a pile of cubes.

Between THE CHUMP CHAMP and DROOPY'S GOOD DEED, two more from the same pattern, Spike gets bashed with a tree, flushed down a waterfall, eaten by beavers, burned to a cinder, blasted to a smudge, and cracked into tiny pieces like a china figurine, and each time it's his own fault for being the villain.

THE THREE LITTLE PUPS is the only cartoon in the world dar-ing enough to stand little Droopy up against an equally lackadaisical villain, in the form of a slowpoke dogcatcher with a Carolina accent who gets all the laughs without going to all lengths and breadths to do it. The action in the film sort of erupts unintentionally, out of strange sources like the hand puppet of a kitten the dogcatcher tries to snare the dogs with ("Meow! Meow! Meow! Meow, man!"), which takes off like a shot after the toy mouse that Droopy tries to snare the kitten with, and drags the dogcatcher on a reluctant trip through several backyards. "If this don't work," says the Carolina hound of his final scheme, "I'll . . . I'll go into television!" The scheme doesn't work, and within three seconds he has gotten himself into the movie Droopy is watching on television. In the incredible final shot, the animated dogcatcher swings into view riding a live-action horse and steals the scene again.

But the pièce de résistance of Droopy's career, and a handsome enough entry for anybody's pedigree, is DRAG-A-LONG DROOPY, of 1954. Here the villain is Avery's old standby, The Wolf (no other name is provided), who devotes half his footage to various unsuccessful attempts at getting on his horse: falling on his face in the dirt, playing leap-frog with the dumb animal, and finally sliding with the saddle to a spot underneath the horse's ribcage. The best routine in the film is one of the best in the world. Avery builds it up in good, methodical, silent-comedy fashion, and then uses as his topper one of those insane gags out of nowhere that only he can do. The Wolf, in an upstairs room in a one-horse-town saloon, hops out the window and onto the porch in hot pursuit of an escaped Droopy, and hops from there onto his one horse—or toward his one horse, as he ends up landing on his chin just to one side of it. For his second try, he dashes, determined, into the saloon again, runs out the second-story window, leaps off the porch, and bites the dust in exactly the same spot. Getting wise now, he moves the horse over to where he keeps breaking his teeth, then runs into the saloon again, out the second-story window again, off the porch again, and onto his head in exactly the spot the horse was standing before. Tiring of this, he gives up and calls a cab. As a climax to a beautifully constructed routine, this comes as both unexpected and inevitable.

The plot concerns the familiar struggle between the ranchers and the sheepherders, taken to unfamiliar dimensions like the opening track across the Bear Butte Ranch: cattle to the left of you, cattle to the right of you, cattle on the homestead, cattle in the living room, cattle on the dinner table, cattle on the front porch, cattle hanging around on the roof. The cattleman, catching our wondering eyes, observes, "You know, uh, I raise cattle." In all this nonsense, Droopy can hardly be accused of doing anything at all—even to the point of sitting there like a bump on a noggin, reading a comic book, while his enterprising pistols carry on the shoot-out for him—a perfect image for Droopy's contribution to the remarkable films he was the almost incidental star of.

A Couple of Gems

The best of Avery's cartoons for MGM don't even pretend to have an interesting character in them—just the usual assortment of nondescript cats and dogs and unctuous narrators that offer no interference to the director's owlish eye. It is an extremely arbitrary cat who opens 1947's KING-SIZE CANARY looking for food in a back alley in the middle of the night. But two nearby boxes come to his aid when he tries to crawl inside a kitchen window. Stacked on top of each other, they still aren't high enough to let him in, but anxiously, desperately, he stacks them on top of the space they took up when they were stacked on top of each other, as if there were four boxes there, and they give him plenty of leeway and he scrambles in. The two boxes hang suspended in air for a half-beat, then, the anxiety gone, they collapse, spent, to the ground. Like the baseball bat in EARLY BIRD DOOD IT which wilts in proportion to the dismay experienced by the bird who is holding it, the boxes demonstrate that the laws of nature in Avery's universe are determined by the mood of the moment. The cat may not have much personality, but for a couple of old boxes these guys are real charmers.

The foray for food uncovers nothing but a threadbare kitchen, and one mouse sitting in a cat food can who protests that it would be imprudent of the cat to eat him just now, as he, the mouse, has seen KING-SIZE CANARY before, and knows that he saves the cat's life in the end. "But there's a mighty tempting canary in the next room," says the mouse, "eat HIM!" Then the canary turns out to be about as juicy as a raisin.

And this is where the central hub of a good Avery hyperbole begins to roll: the subconscious acceptance of a notion we know perfectly well to be wholly senseless. Avery cartoons probably wouldn't be able to function if it weren't for a whole team of crazy ideas that we insist on holding dear to our heads, all the while knowing that we would have to be idiots to really believe them. Once we have accepted the conventional cartoon world of hobo cats who need a shave and talking mice who have seen the movie before, then he can lead us to the main bypass—the little bottle of Jumbo-Gro, one of those patented absurdities adorned with before and after drawings of a withered flower on the left and a sturdy, healthy flower on the right. Consciously, we are aware of this drawing as a device; we realize its presence on the label bears no relation to the potency of the liquid inside. Otherwise, we would be morons. But subconsciously we will be subtly convinced that a miracle is somehow contained in the bottle, that this is an elixir worth spending money on. Otherwise, the advertising industry would have disintegrated eons ago. It's just the fact that Avery uses, as the premise from which everything else takes off, a commercial product of the kind we have sold to us every day, rather than some fantasied "magic potion" we could only swallow against our better judgment, that makes the ensuing farcical situations seem so tangible and real.

After a brainstorm (which rains all over the table), the cat pours Jumbo-Gro down the bird's throat, hoping he can nurture the hapless withered thing into the semblance of a duck, or a goose, or, hell, maybe even a pheasant. His success is extraordinary. Before he can take the first bite out of the leg, there, sitting on the plate on the table before him, has sprouted a giant, seven-foot yellow ox. At that, the cat vanishes in retreat, while the innocent canary spends some time getting properly adjusted to the fact that he's an ox now and gathering up the wherewithal to chase him. The stray bottle of Jumbo-Gro then goes on to enjoy a lengthy career of being tested out by a random sampling of neighborhood pets, each of whom suddenly discovers in himself an unmanageable potential for turning into a monster. There is a double take every

Model sheet for KING-SIZE CANARY (1947) with important details noted.

87

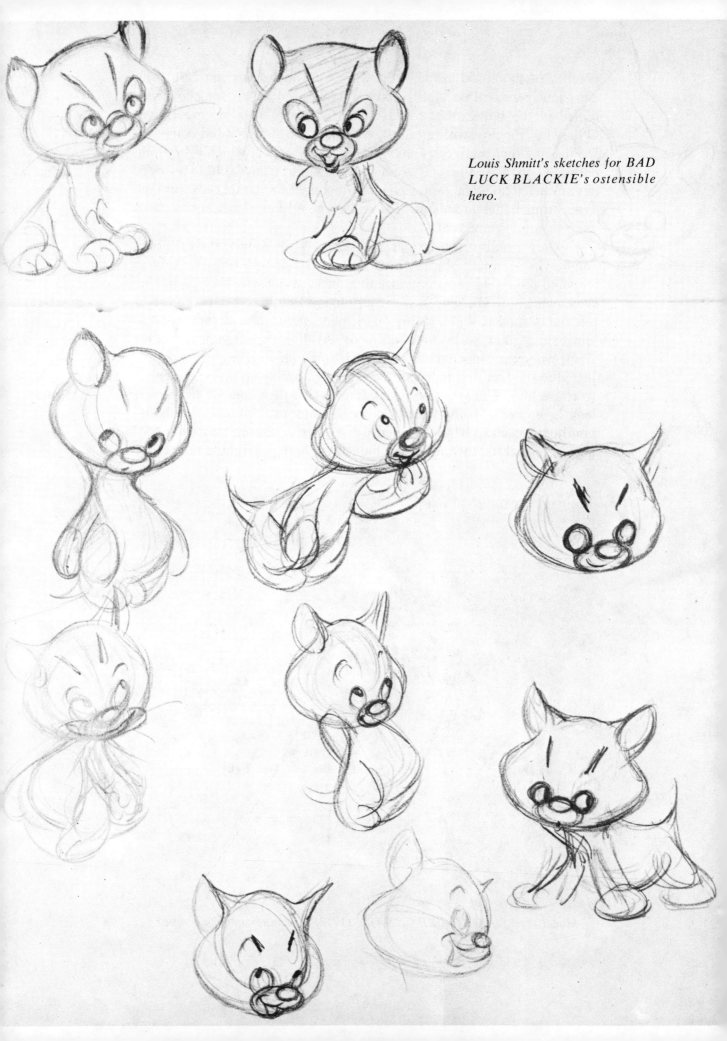

Louis Shmitt's sketches for BAD LUCK BLACKIE's ostensible hero.

instant, as one of the animals stops and comprehends that some new giant is here to be contended with. A bird the size of an elephant is chased by a cat the size of a truck, until they both stop and meet a woolly mammoth dog the size of a house. (And this is all from one bottle of the stuff. Which was half-used to begin with.) The stodgiest kind of representational drawing is used to good effect in the backgrounds: here, over houses and garages from a 1940s textbook in accounting, are clambering outlandish creatures out of some dietician's nightmare. The sun has come up by this time, and the chases extend downtown, where the four-story dog is hot on the trail of the two-story cat. Until they get to the corner and meet a seven-story mouse.

So it came to pass. The mouse did save the cat's life. (Although if he had really seen the cartoon before he must have realized his alibi was only half true, that there would have been no need to save the cat's life if he had just let himself be eaten. There also would have been no cartoon. Creative, that mouse.) All this does is reduce the battle to a struggle for survival between the cat and the mouse, both of them grabbing the bottle of Jumbo-Gro from each other, sprouting into the clouds at every swallow, and stampeding all over the known universe. Off they go, one Gargantuan cat chasing one behemoth mouse, traversing whole states in a couple of paces, charging across the Grand Canyon in one leap and one bound, feverishly swallowing Jumbo-Gro until the bottle runs out, then turning and explaining to us that the movie's over, embracing each other like pals, standing, two incredible giants, either one of them twice the size of the Earth, and both attempting to maintain a precarious balance on the skimpy planet, waving sweetly at the camera as it pulls back to the viewpoint of Saturn to get the whole thing in frame. Gradually, carefully, we have been led in a logical progression from one common, well-accepted absurdity, on into the outward regions of an absurd universe.

The same careful progression is a hallmark of another acknowledged Avery jewel, BAD LUCK BLACKIE, of 1949. Here we're dealing not with commercialism, but with "superstition," that outmoded set of irrational notions whose medieval foundations and physical irrelevance are well within our intellectual grasp. But that doesn't stop us from reacting, if involuntarily, to these survivals of past religions. There are very few buildings with a thirteenth floor, or motels with a Room Thirteen. (Texas, by the way, is crawling with such folk myths, all the way from a spider in your bedroom being a sign of good luck to a vision of your eventual spouse appearing before you at the inspiration of a thimbleful of salt.) So if a black cat crosses your path you're in trouble. OK.

BAD LUCK BLACKIE kicks off with a short sequence of unbelievable cruelty, and just about the only instance of Avery violence that is actually painful. A vicious old dog is mercilessly maltreating a defenseless kitten, catching his tongue on a mousetrap in his milk, swallowing him and disgorging him again, that sort of thing. This is also one of the few cases of an Avery character successfully tugging at our heartstrings, and with an infallible comic sense Avery has managed to make this painful spectacle an amusing (if uncomfortable) scene—mostly by punctuating it with the dog's genial-malicious wheezy chortle, so that we laugh, not at the horrible gags perpetrated on the kitten, but at the dog's warped notion that this is a funny thing to do.

A black cat comes to the rescue and, purely out of an altruistic love for cathood, sets up a deal with the kitten. Any time the kitten blows on an ordinary household whistle, the black cat will cross the old bulldog's path. In return, the kitten will do nothing. That's the deal. The first test of the arrangement turns up in just a few seconds. Accompanied by a sprightly rendition of "Comin' Through the Rye," the black cat makes a mysterious entrance, dances in front of the dog, and makes a mysterious exit. And then, before you have time to get apprehensive about it, a flower pot has come crashing down on the dog's head. (The camera ascending to a slightly Olympian, sort of cosmic viewpoint to contain the catastrophe, then scooting down to a kitten's-eye view for the conclusion of the negotiation.) So far, no problem. A flower pot can fall from a window any time, and we're just expecting to see this villainous dog get beaned about now, black cat's entrance or no. There is only the split-second timing of the two events to make this peculiar enough to be funny. But when this happens every time the whistle is blown and the black cat appears, and the flower pot is quickly followed by another flower pot, then a heavy trunk, a small bomb, a cash register, four horse-shoes (and a horse, looking extremely puzzled), a fire hydrant, a safe, enough bricks to form a wall (which they do), and then an anvil, we

begin to suspect that there's something up there, and it's not happy with that dog.

We all know how any other director would have handled this situation. Cut away to a construction site, and a closeup of a sign saying "Danger: Falling Objects. Keep Away!" Then a rope snapping on a girder, followed by an aghast foreman hollering, "The rope's broken! Run for your life!" and a panic-stricken crowd fleeing the scene. Then, after that, maybe, the dog could stray into the area and meet his doom.

Not Tex Avery. A few bars of "Comin' Through the Rye," and CRASH! the dog is clobbered. When Avery described this cartoon to me, several months before I had a chance to see it, it was with the accustomed amiable glee that precluded the idea of any damage being done to anybody. "The black cat would no sooner cross the dog's path," he told me, "Than WHAM! he'd be hit with a safe or something." "Where does the safe come from?" I asked innocently, and not without naïveté. Avery's answer was a small stammer and a vigorous waving of the hand, as if I had asked the most irrelevant question in the world. Which, in a sense, I had.

In the mechanical inevitability of these falling objects, in their escalating impact, in the wonderful absurdity that unites such illogical events with such seeming logic, the question of where the things may be coming from becomes totally irrelevant. They *have* to be there. The lampoon on a popular superstition can be taken just so far, and only when it's coupled with this steadily increasing sense of vengeance is it capable of producing such perfect comic violence and the odd intuitive idea that fate is taking its inevitable course in dumping things on the dog. We begin to be convinced the whole cosmos has ganged up on him. (The dog, of course, reacts to having some of the heaviest objects that exist in the world falling from an unseen source, perhaps miles away, with a force strong enough to shatter granite, by being nonplused, and somewhat tipsy. At one point his head is blown away, and it takes him a whole fadeout to get it back again.)

As if the main thread of the situation were not hilarity enough, it is embroidered with every variety of character interplay as a cat-and-dog game is played out by the principals, astounding us with: 1) the kitten's resourcefulness in finding new hiding places, 2) the bulldog's resourcefulness in getting the kitten in impossible spots, 3) the cat's own brand of resourcefulness that tops both of them, appearing out of one place he couldn't possibly be and disappearing into another where he couldn't possibly go, and 4) the cosmos' latest answer to the continuing hostilities.

But, grand as it all works out for the cosmos, the divine retribution notion isn't complete until the kitten can get his own licks in. A nearby mopful of white paint cancels out the black cat, and "Comin' Through the Rye" heralds nothing. While the dog takes his chance to engage in some fiendish torture with the white (nee black) cat, the kitten sees a chance to cover himself with black paint and perform his own strutting.

At the same time, the full importance of the whistle has been grasped by the apocalyptic fate who's been wreaking all this havoc. Fate has come to learn, like one of Pavlov's more misbegotten beasts, to respond simply to the sound of a whistle. When the dog accidentally swallows it, and every hiccup gives birth to a toot, and you're already aware that he's been hit with everything but the kitchen sink, fate answers with the kitchen sink. Then a bathtub. Then a piano. And then, with a hiccuptweet-THUD, there's a rapid culmination of all the operating threads, as fate becomes more vindictive, more absurd, and more resourceful all at once, smashing the dog with a steamroller, a passenger plane, a Greyhound bus, and, as a coup de grace, the *S.S. Arizona*.

Cosmic viewpoint again. He is just a speck on the horizon by this time, and it is clearly implied that this is the last time he will ever be so bold as to tangle with a kitten.

Not a word is spoken in the final fadeout. Simply the white cat shaking hands with the black kitten and a heart-warming rendition of "Auld Lang Syne." Then a close-up of the black kitten. And he chuckles, as menacingly as the bulldog. And for the first time we realize that the cruelty so horrifying at the beginning of the film has been reproduced a hundredfold, and we have been absolutely delighted at it. We should have known Avery wasn't going to let his kitten be too lovable for too long. Our allegiances have migrated all the way from sympathy for the tormented to sheer glee at the tormentor. We have been brought full circle to the transformation of an innocent into a diabolic. And it's been an amazing journey.

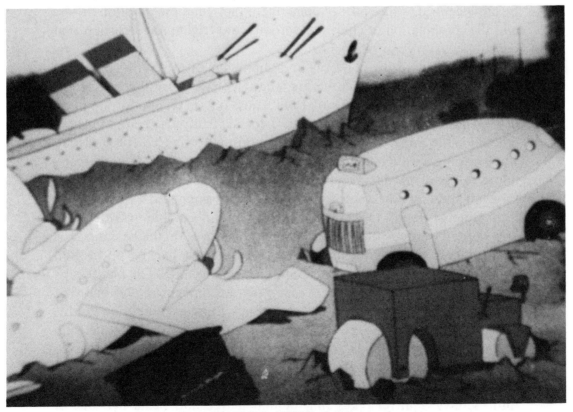

BAD LUCK BLACKIE: the aftermath.

Sex and Violence

The best absurdity, of course, springs from a hard core of reality, and in the presence of a reality as powerful and pervasive as that old demon sex, Avery has a chance to perform miracles. The knots of sexual anxieties, fevers, and inhibitions into which we are willing to tie ourselves have been explored fully and brilliantly in obsessionist studies like Hitchcock's VERTIGO, Kubrick's LOLITA, and Buñuel's EL, but Avery, with his comic relief, manages to gaily untie the knots in a series of dizzying orgies of sexual frenzy no child should be allowed to see. The hyperbole in this case is strictly Aristophanic, and bears a boiling blood relation to the Dionysian phallic rites all comedy is rooted in. Nothing could be more central to the spirit of comedy, in fact, than the question of sex, and the combination of charming ferocity and frightening delirium that constitutes Avery's answer.

Like many of the concerns and characters of the MGM films, the sexual frenzy begins within the first year. Avery's third film for MGM, RED HOT RIDING HOOD, of 1943, starts out, in true-to-form parody of the Harman and Ising style, with a tootsie-fruitsie narrator gushing out, "Good evening, kiddies! Once upon a time Little Red Riding Hood was skipping through the wood! She was going to her grandmother's house to take Grandma a basket of nice goodies!" He doesn't get very far with these goodies before the wolf, who's supposed to pounce on Red Riding Hood, turns around with an unbeatable world-weary, angry-sad, Toshiro Mifune expression, and pounces on the narrator. His plea for deliverance from this pablum treatment is backed up by Red Riding Hood's, and finally even Grandma chimes in, "I'm plenty sick of it myself!" (This is one of Avery's favorite openings, and one that has a number of variations, including Bugs Bunny reading the credits of TORTOISE BEATS HARE and throwing a fit over the title, and the adorable squirrel who opens up SCREWBALL SQUIRREL explaining that this is to be a cartoon "about me and all my friends in the forest: Charlie Chipmunk, Wallace Woodchuck, Barney Bear . . ." until Screwy Squirrel takes him behind a tree and beats hell out of him.) Whereupon the action shifts to Grandma's penthouse (with a neon sign flashing "COME UP AND SEE ME SOMETIME") and

the Hollywood nightclub where Red Riding Hood works ("30 Gorgeous Girls—No Cover").

The wolf becomes a zoot-suited, chain-swinging, two-mile-long-car-driving Hollywood hipster wolf, a sort of caricature of a popular expression. (And, as always in Avery, the unabashed crudity is a simultaneous celebration and satire.) The wolf loses all the cool he is given when he catches sight of Red Riding Hood doing her "Hey, Daddy!" number. He howls, whistles, stomps, claps, loses his eyeballs, pounds on the table with his fists and with a chair, smashes himself on the head with whatever's handy, and otherwise finds noise so necessary he must employ a whistling, stomping, and clapping machine to keep up with his excitement. (The movement of the dancing Miss Ridinghood is worth getting excited about, too, not only for the obvious reasons, but because her sprightly animation is being performed without benefit of Rotoscope or even live-action footage for study. The animation of humans is a tricky business, and in a medium more adaptable to rubber-limbed ducks and wisecracking rabbits, the wriggling of Avery's bouncy starlets serves as a joyful beacon to the world, and a shining example to shame the plasticized, programmed impersonalities of Disney's heroes and heroines.)

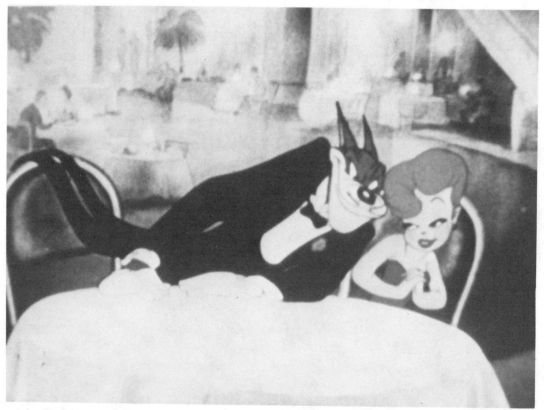

Red is too much the worldly-wise princess to fall for the Wolf's line in RED HOT RIDING HOOD (1943).

The wolf chases Red clear to Grandma's, only to make the discovery that Grandmother sports as equally active a libido as he does and, all of a sudden, just as much energy. The chase that now ensues—the wolf frantically dashing for exits that persist in disappearing, and engaging in desperate footraces through a parody of MGM penthouses that seems to cover acres—gets us catastrophically close to a direct reverse of the original story, in the shape of Grandma eating the wolf.

RED HOT RIDING HOOD is a nice film, one capable of knocking an audience on its heels and elsewhere, and a genuine delight to the uninhibited and the over-inhibited who prefer such honest hysteria to the fairy tales we're usually handed. And yet it's only a come-on for what's to follow.

THE SHOOTING OF DAN McGOO, 1945, takes the idea further and mingles it with several other forms of Avery comedy. A burlesque (in both senses) of (and Avery's second stab at) Robert Service's serviceable poem, it will take a line like "A bunch of the boys were whooping it up in the Malamute Saloon," and turn it into an excuse to stage a hundred versions of THE SPOILERS going on at once: a tumultuous cacophony of whooping and hollering, dancing and gunfighting, somersaulting, hallooing, strangling, kicking, running, machine-gunning, drinking, wailing, carousing, and any other unseemly and unlikely behavior capable of being jammed into one frame.

One of those two-mile-long cars pulls into the town (Coldernell, Alaska), depositing our friend the wolf, who makes his entrance as a snowman. He sidles up to the bar and demands, "Straight whiskey!" He takes a good heady swallow, and immediately his extremities make determined attempts at splattering him all over the map of February, succeeding in sending him around the ceiling beams and down into the floorboard, where he leaps to his feet in time to complain to the bartender, "This stuff's been cut!"

The "Lady that's known as Lou" gets introduced as the stripper sensation of the joint, and she does one rousing chorus of "Put Your Arms Around Me, Wolfie, Hold Me Tight," which rouses the wolf no end. He threatens to melt the whole polar ice cap with his reactions, which include chomping away at a nearby pillar too ravenously to ever notice that it is not a giant carrot. He makes a grab for Lady Lou, but all he gets is her goat, and it's phlegmatic Droopy who emerges triumphant in the end. But the fadeout can't arrive before he's had his share of whoops and hollers and carryings-on in direct imitation of the villain he's just demolished.

In these pictures, the guy who loses his head over some girl, and most of his other bodily parts in the process, is usually smashed to pieces, or put away through some more euphemistic process, to provide the moral retribution. But morality in a comedy exists only to be denied, and the guy is only put away to prove that the carryings-on can carry right on without him.

Another fairy tale gets the wise-ass treatment in SWING SHIFT CINDERELLA, 1945, in which Grandma's magic power enables the young starlet Cinderella to enter the twentieth century ("You do wave a mean wand," she's told) and perform in a posh nightclub (which advertises "Fights Nightly"), where her "Oh, Wolfie" routine ("Oh, Wolfie! Oh, Wolfie! Ain't you the one!") drives the wolf up the wall. Grandma also has the power to equip herself with a spiffy motor scooter,

WILD AND WOOLFY (1945).

Little Eva from UNCLE TOM'S CABANA (1947).

and her clamorous, throaty growl reverberating madly through her apartment, she drives the wolf even further up all four walls.

The sexual furor makes a return in WILD AND WOOLFY, 1945 again, surrounded by the elements of a Droopy Western. UNCLE TOM'S CABAÑA, 1947, provides a lot more laughs and goes to great lengths in all directions at once. Uncle Tom is a grand old black man (not so much a caricature as a parody of a caricature), seen informing a crowd of knee-high listeners of his contretemps with Simon Legree. He first impresses them with a series of personification gags, demonstrating how Mr. Legree ("Old Ladies Tripped; Kittens Drowned") was (literally) two-faced, a snake, and rolling in dough (one of these at a time), while starvation stared Uncle Tom in the face (in the form of a grisly old green ghoul morosely fixated on him). The swinger in this case is Little Eva, whose "penthouse" is a full-sized Tara mounted on the top of a skyscraper. Eva becomes the star attraction in the swinging nightclub ("No Dogs Allowed; Wolves Welcome") ol' Tom fashions out of his tiny cabin, and, in the calculated caprice we have come to expect in these cartoons, the minuscule shack is soon surrounded by a two-acre parking lot jammed full of automobiles and seven mobs of customers patiently waiting outside for their turn.

The sex-kitten purrs of Little Eva and her rendition of "Carry Me Back to Old Virginny" send Simon Legree into what must be at once the most graphic and the least suggestive images of erotic fascination ever presented. He starts innocently enough by sailing straight up, ass first, to the tones of the music. He shakes a stalk of celery over the saltshaker, and munches on the saltshaker. He butters his knuckles and chews both arms past the elbow. Coolly, he lights his nose; then, extending the metaphor, he takes his nose off and crushes it out in the ashtray. Presented with a whole pie, he cuts a large slice out of the table and devours it. These are the *tame* reactions. Only after these are done is he permitted to go whole hog and eat the crockery, shatter it over his head, smother himself in ketchup, and brain himself repeatedly with the dinner table.

The energy that's been worked up this way is expended for us by Mr. Legree in an all-out war with Uncle Tom that serves as a climax upon a climax. Avery was smart enough, after RED HOT RIDING HOOD, to move the sexual arousal sequence to the end of the film, where it could bring everything to a suitably noisy finish. Now he's developed the sexual arousal to a high point in comedy barely suggested by its primitive beginnings in that early film, and the challenge of having to follow it with something better is formidable indeed. But this he does, in a Tex Avery apotheosis of wild storytelling that has Uncle Tom fastened to a powder keg, riddled with machine gun bullets, thrown off a cliff, fed to an alligator, smashed with an overgrown mallet, tied to the railroad tracks and run over, and tossed into a sawmill and split in two. (Bloodlessly, painlessly. Not even the drawing style suffers.) Finally there is some yardage up the "Umpire State Building," concluded by Uncle Tom's being thrown off. "I fall down fourteen miles and hit on the pavement," he tells us, "and right there is where

I gets mad!" His revenge for these horrors is to pick up the Umpire State Building with his bare hands and hurl it and Simon Legree over the moon and into the Pacific Ocean.

Uncle Tom's audience, contrary youths that they are, are at pains to believe this story. "If'n it ain't the truth, I hope that lightnin' come down and strike me dead," solemnly intones the storyteller—whereupon lightning does come down and do exactly that, in a combination extension of the story and retribution for it, sending Uncle Tom blissfully off to that paradise specifically reserved for great tellers of tall tales.

LITTLE 'TINKER, 1948, is next on the list of orgies, and most likely the most unusual of the bunch. The story concerns a lonely skunk and his search for love, an idea perhaps borrowed from Chuck Jones and his first two Pepe Le Pew cartoons—except that the timid, shy, sensitive main character of LITTLE 'TINKER is a far cry from Jones' brash, overconfident Le Pew, and, besides, Avery has sprinkled more gags into this one tiny cartoon than you will find in all of Jones' fine expansive series. It's a curious examination of how many funny gags can spring from an unfunny idea, as we watch the gradations of reaction on the rabbits and squirrels in this sympathetic skunk's vicinity, the flowers instantly withering as he passes, the fish sprouting feet for the purpose of vacating the lake—all leading up to the wise old owl who never makes a reaction, never even opens his eyes, just keels over, unconscious. It's also a neat example of how sympathy can be wrung from our hearts without making any apparent attempt at it.

Following the advice of a book on love he's been handed, the skunk dresses up as a Frank Sinatra imitation (accomplished principly by the reduction of his body to the diameter of telephone cord), and puts on a public serenade of "All or Nothing at All." With an eagerness and an intensity that is positively frightening, forty million rabbits spring up out of their burrows, holler "Frankie!", and begin driving themselves crazy over the sight of him, hopping around, sailing through the air, and smashing each other over the head with each other. Which constitutes in my mind one of the most devious gems of gag transferral in the history of comedy. Attributing sexual desperation to a horny old wolf, after all, is enough of a sacred coup in the cartoon world; passing it on to a litter of adorable little bunny rabbits is one of the most vicious, un-Disneyfied gags Avery ever perpetrated. What is also interesting is the way in which the song sequence, usually played relatively straight, is made to be another figure of fun, so that a non-stop montage is derived by intercutting young Frank Sinatra lampoons (standing behind the microphone stand and being obscured by it; slipping through a knothole in the stage and disappearing from sight) with frenzied libido gags (little rabbits beating little rabbits with little rabbits; one priceless image of fertility where a female snuggles up to a sapling and it eagerly responds by sprouting a full head of leaves).

When, finally, disguised as a fox, the fellow finds his own true love (another skunk disguised as a fox), he neatly deposits the useless book on love outside the cartoon (on the other side of the red heart that closes in instead of the iris, leaving them in privacy), providing Avery with one of his most beautiful endings, and one that keeps his faith in lunacy alive while tempering his fiendish delight at the excesses of the wolf with a note of tenderness.

After six years and six films, after developing one gag into a routine, building up the routine to an exorbitant height, and then adding a touching footnote to it, you would think that would be just about it. You would think he would have depleted his natural supply of sex gags and that anything coming after this would bear the pallor of strain and repetition. But no, it turns out this has only been so much buildup, so much enticement to take the thing even further. In 1949 Avery comes out with LITTLE RURAL RIDING HOOD, and not only does it put all the previous sex cartoons to shame, it does so without repeating a single gag from any of them. Like Harold Lloyd dangling on the side of his skyscraper in five different films, he has found the one situation so rich and full of potential that he can go on mining the same ore without a sign of ever running out.

Again we open up with a pretense of telling the story straight. Country bumpkin, adolescent Red Riding Hood (an ungainly creature one soon wishes to see speedily eaten) tells us she's on her way to her grandmother's house. But waiting in Grandma's bed is a country bumpkin wolf, explaining to us that his intentions are not to eat the approaching creature, but (in his words) to "chase her and catch her and kiss her and hug her and love her and hug her and kiss her and hug her...," providing a disturbingly full illustration of his desires by writhing around on the bed with a blanket. But Red doesn't surrender too easily, and in the ensuing galloping around, the wolf is once split in half horizontally by colliding with a French door, and once transformed into a swinging door dissected vertically. Now, this kind of ribald physical distortion within the first minute of one of Avery's cartoons is a sure indication that there's great stuff to come. His talent for building one gag and one sequence upon another is too good to keep this from being an early giveaway.

The massive master shot that immediately follows is comedy enough for the finale of any normal cartoon. One poor victimized door is slammed in and around a single room, helplessly creating doorways everywhere it lands, while Red Riding Hood and the wolf appear at each new entry to slam the door anew, creating more. It's hard to believe that one door could have so many careers, but not much harder than the multiplicity of wolves and Red Riding Hoods that seem to have appeared to keep up the momentum. (The talent of all Avery characters for dividing at random is matched by their ability to multiply without limit like amoebae and improper fractions.)

The commotion is halted by a telegram from the wolf's city cousin, telling him to come to the city, where the Red Riding Hoods are plentiful and the hunting is good. A picture of one is enclosed, and after the wolf has indicated his approval by flying into several pieces,

Sexual enthusiasm in LITTLE RURAL RIDING HOOD (1949).

stretching his eyeballs from the ceiling to the floor, dropping his tongue to his shoes, and stomping his feet on his own head, he leaps in his jalopy and takes off for the city.

Once there, he proceeds to shatter all known laws of Newtonian physics and Einsteinian relativity, searching his cousin's apartment and most of the adjoining apartments for the girl he's been promised, and, with one clobber, a baseball bat suddenly materializes, silencing both the wolf and the soundtrack. The city cousin, an ultra-smoothie who never bats an eyelash or opens an eye, informs the wolf, with a voice dripping from the back of his larynx, that "Miss Riding Hood is not here. We will meet her this evening at the club. But remember, here in the city we do not shout and whistle at the ladies."

This advice proves all for naught as they arrive at "the club," the city wolf in an icy demeanor that seems to suit the place, the country wolf climbing all over himself with excitement, his head and limbs revolving around his body like idling propellers, keeping up an unceasing babble of "Girls, girls, where's the girls, wanna kiss the girls, where's the girls, sure do love girls!" The city's version of Miss Riding Hood is our old favorite from all the previous entries, performing a reprise of her big hit, "Oh, Wolfie," from SWING SHIFT CINDER-ELLA (an economy measure probably necessitated by the exorbitant nature of the rest of the film).

From here on in, it's the old expression-repression routine, with the city wolf and his infuriating placid exterior doing his best to silence all of his country cousin's yokel yodels. One's eyes pop out, and when the other's hands rush forth to preserve decorum, the disembodied eyes slip, determined, through the fingers, repeatedly, each time they present themselves, whish-POP-whish-POP-whish-POP, forever. The city wolf invites endless contortions and extortions, as all his attempts to jam his troublesome cousin's noisy face into untroublesome places like sleeves simply result in heads, arms, and whistles emerging from unsuspected spots on his own anatomy. The country wolf puffs feverishly on a cigarette, which makes an ash of itself, and his wolfish proboscis in the bargain, leaving both to crumble off and abandon the two undiverted eyes who remain as survivors.

When this whole destruction and restoration comedy is over, and the girl finishes her song, the country wolf, accompanied by a plethora of horse whinnies, streetcar bells, stomping sounds, percussion effects, and any other stray noises hanging around the sound department, rushes pell-mell toward the stage—only to be stopped by a mallet strung in his suspenders, and wheeled, squeaking, back to the car.

But the city wolf's aggravating reservation, like the morality in the previous films, exists only to be ridiculed, and when he gets his chance to explode it's on a much more idiotic pretext. Having driven the country wolf home to remove him from the pressures of city life, he catches sight of the adolescent bumpkin who opened the film and goes to pieces over her. This gives the country cousin a chance to stash his exhausted relative into the car and charge back to the city again, thus proving that sex, wild reactions, and sound and fury are eternal.

This brings to a trim little end one of the highlights of Avery's career, sharing a space alongside WHO KILLED WHO?, BAD LUCK BLACKIE, DRAG-A-LONG DROOPY, and a few others, as one of the greatest treasures of comic mayhem in the world.

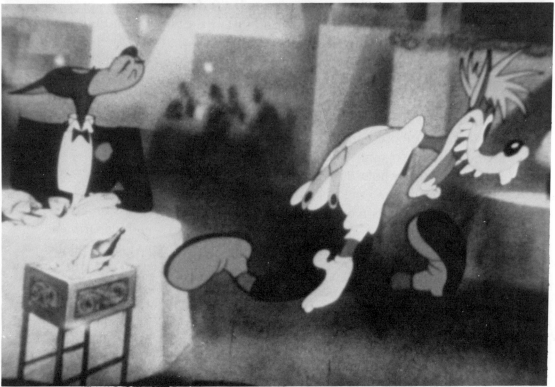

Character contrast: reading from left to right, the City Wolf and the Country Wolf in LITTLE RURAL RIDING HOOD.

106

Iris Out

The late forties and early fifties are rich in just this sort of fourth-dimensional acrobatics, and from THE CAT THAT HATED PEOPLE, in 1948, to DROOPY'S GOOD DEED in 1951, Avery presents us with eighteen beautifully handled cartoons in a row, not a letdown among them. By this time, he has progressed from the self-conscious zaniness of Screwy Squirrel into a more languid lunacy that flips reality on its ear with an ease that is seemingly effortless. Avery's style has finally caught up with his sense of humor.

The obstreperous Spike engages in a furious set of contests, not only with Droopy, but with every stray cat, bear, gopher, and chicken in Avery's menagerie. In COUNTERFEIT CAT his tongue is unrolled clear across the living room by a neighborhood feline, who, in his en-enthusiasm, has mistaken it for a bird. In GARDEN GOPHER, he

COUNTERFEIT CAT (1949).

107

cracks into pieces like china again, this time to reveal that it takes four little Spikes to make up one big one. In VENTRILOQUIST CAT he endures an explosion while floating aloft on a kite, and as he stands surveying his vanished midsection, an apathetic duck wings his way by and sails directly between him.

COUNTERFEIT CAT (1949).

But Spike is about the only recurring character in a gallery of garrulous gorgons. ROCK-A-BYE BEAR is the story of Joe Bear, of Big Bear, California, a noisy old curmudgeon who can't stand noise, attempting hibernation in a cave concealed behind curtains in the back of his spacious split-level home. At any indiscreet peep emitted by a subsidiary character, he emerges from the cave with a round of good sound effects, stomping on the floor till the furnishings bounce, and hollering, "Shut up! Quiet! I said Quiet!" His annoyance is apparently limited to peeps, it turns out, because his house is demolished in the course of the action, with whooping explosives and flaming skyrockets, and reduced to a charred and scabrous heap, but this he sleeps through.

THE CAT THAT HATED PEOPLE concerns an astutely misanthropic cat who suffers endless unwarranted indignities like being jammed inside a milk bottle, frustrating his attempts to steal it (and, perversely, any attempt to protect it). He complains that disagreeable human beings are apt to "step on ya, walk on ya, step on ya, walk on ya," while an agreeable sidewalk crowd accompanies his remarks with a demonstration. "And kick ya!" adds the cat as a footnote, whereupon he gets booted out of the frame. The simplest solution is to take off for the moon, where he meets up with a gag concept borrowed from Clampett's picture PORKY IN WACKYLAND, and borrowed

108

all over again for Disney's ALICE IN WONDERLAND and George Dunning's YELLOW SUBMARINE: autonomous lipsticks, fiendish sharpeners attacking innocent pencils, and an aimless watering can who sprouts the old cat from the turf in the shape of a tulip. This angers the earthling just enough and there is only one thing to do: he provides himself with a golf course backdrop, sets himself up on a tee, and swats himself away with a golf club. This effectively returns him to the earth, where he hugs the sidewalk like it was a patchwork quilt and returns to getting stepped on.

In FIELD AND SCREAM a flock of ducks answers a hunter's duck call by turning around with delighted grins and honking their own duck calls back at him. In CAR OF TOMORROW we are promised a new design sporting a "magnificent rear end," and Avery turns out to have extended personification beyond even the limits we expected him to maintain. In LUCKY DUCKY there is absolute silence when a tiny duckling and the two hunters in pursuit of him suddenly find themselves and their surroundings in ashen shades of gray. Out of curiosity, they retrace their steps to a demarcation line labeled "Technicolor Ends Here." And they exit screen left, in the domain of the greens and the purples.

THE FLEA CIRCUS, 1954, can boast the wittiest opening sequence of the bunch, and clear, if unnecessary, proof that Avery can incite appreciable hysteria without even suggesting any violence. The flea circus is just like any other circus, except that a magnifying glass comes with the price of admission, so that when the curtain goes up on the perfectly ordinary vaudeville stage you can divine some semblance of entertainment out of the tiny dots that proceed to cavort upon it. First on the bill is a full-scale marching band, consisting of

Model sheet for THE CAT THAT HATED PEOPLE *(1948), the title who could not make up its mind.*

The rabbit in DOGGONE TIRED, as designed by Louis Shmitt.

twenty or thirty fleas parading around in formation, sounding out some brassy Sousa tune. A bundle of tumbling spots called acrobats appear, as well as a minuscule classical pianist, and then a microscopic tap dancer who gets in a couple of licks on "Way Down Upon the Swanee River" and disappears through a knothole. Least popular is a clown, whose audience response is indicated by a horrendous shot of two hundred fifty giant scowls, all emphasized with magnifying glasses. A life-size stage hook appears and whisks the flea offstage. Most uncanny of all is the grand finale, a stupendous Busby Berkeley rendition of a gay old song called "La France" by a talented mob of one hundred fifty shapely young chorus fleas prancing about on a giant (knee-high) five-level platform. But the hulabaloo comes to a halt when a dog happens backstage, and with a gasp and the sound of a buffalo stampede, the entire cast of the grand finale high-tails it off stage and onto this poor terrified mongrel, who is left to dash hither and yon, uphill and down, through village and farm, past vacant lots and busy buildings, accompanied every damn foot of the way by further choruses of "La France."

There is marvelous comedy in DOGGONE TIRED, 1949, with a hounded hunting dog kept from slumber by a nervy rabbit who is to be his morning's prey. The rabbit, though fighting for his life, is never played up for sympathy or terror—just for the number of crazy gags that can be gotten out of his infinite attempts to make odd noises in the middle of the night. All the gags nurture themselves from meager, prosaic beginnings into wild insidious Avery finishes—like when the rabbit ties the lightswitch to the swinging pendulum of the clock and the dog tries halting the incessant on-again-off-again rhythm by (what else?) swallowing the light bulb whole, but then is left to sit and pout while the on-again-off-again shines brightly onward through his eyes, ears, and nostrils all night.

The dog has lost all patience by the time the rabbit lines him up with a telephone operator, whose tinny voice starts babbling in his ear every line it ever knew: "They do not answer, Long distance, The correct time is 12:00, That number has been disconnected"; and finally, "Oh, Golly!" as the dog grabs the receiver and strangles the innocent operator to death—her tongue protruding from the speaker to give evidence to her demise—and then hangs up on her. Next come a few solid gongs on a fire bell, followed by a good siren imitation, and the dog is up and on his feet with alarm and with the horrifying discovery that roller skates have been strapped to his trusting ankles and he's rolling helplessly across the room, sailing irretrievably out the door, and, from what we can gather from the soundtrack, tumbling up and down innumerable flights of stairs and smashing through one fairground, four construction sites, two bordellos, and an antique shop. DOGGONE TIRED is a fine example of how a plain, ordinary dog-and-rabbit situation can be turned inside-out in Avery's hands, and transformed into a superbly deranged series of physical and logical gyrations. Even when the simplest, most predictable gag is being played, comic delirium is rampant in the treatment.

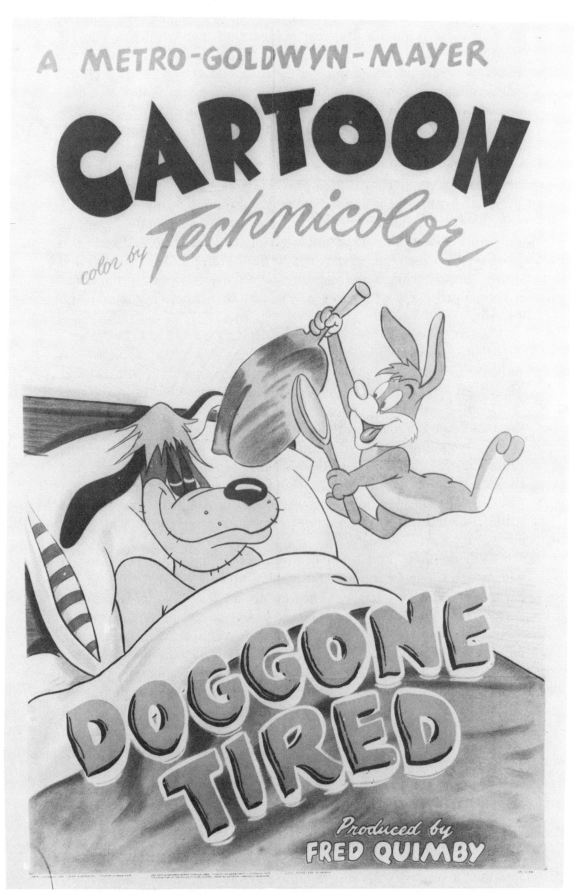

DOGGONE TIRED (1949): MGM's poster artists did their best to imitate the work of Avery's animators, never with complete success.

BILLY BOY, 1954, works the other way around. The situation is one of those good, and sturdy, built-in hyperboles you would never expect to see anywhere but in a Tex Avery cartoon. It's about a goat who eats everything—coffee cups, coffee pots, railroad tracks, farmhouses, automobile innards, globes, everything. He eats the wallpaper off the wall, he eats the skirt off a pin-up, he eats the paper he is drawn on. A patient but firm farmer has found it his task to get rid of the little fellow after he discovers his household swallowed wholesale and his left shoe gobbled away (he has to count the toes on his left foot to be certain he hasn't lost any: two-four-six-eight-ten, they're all there). Tying the goat to a horse, smacking the horse with a broom, and letting it gallop away with its prisoner only results in a sheared and angry horse, who promptly pulls the same trick on the farmer to see how he likes it, and after the farmer gallops away and charges back, it results in a sheared angry farmer, and the two of them stand naked and glaring like plucked chickens.

Animator's sketches for the farmer in BILLY BOY (1954) posed alongside his voracious co-star.

But BILLY BOY suffers. As the fifties wore on, the stylization introduced to the animation medium by UPA and their Mr. Magoo cartoons wound its stylish way into the styles of the major studios. Its effect on Avery cartoons was to loosen up what had by this time evolved into a tight, solid, self-assured personal imagery. The scribbled foliage that passes for trees and the background colors that never quite fit into the outlines they are supposed to fill, all have a felicitous, foot-loose effect which may do fine for the pleasantries of other directors (and furnish, in fact, the heyday of Chuck Jones' career), but here they simply point out how well Avery had coordinated all his elements before this. The bright and sharply defined colors, the synchronized but inappropriate sound effects, the swift and flawless timing, the characters' wholehearted acceptance of the misbegotten world they inhabit, their ontological unity preserved in disintegration, their traits exaggerated to the point of self-parody, their speedy possession of all necessary props and the rapid dissolution of all unnecessary ones, all of these things maintain and make vivid the powerful unreality created in Avery's peak years. Yet they all depend on an acceptance of the one-step-removed cartoon reality of the forties which they can then proceed to demolish. Here, UPA has demolished it for them, and the same activities, launched from a world that is admittedly a false one, have considerably less potency. Avery's own stylization had already developed; he didn't need to be handed somebody else's.

This, as I say, begins to bog down some of the MGM's, but it takes its heaviest toll in the handful of Walter Lantz cartoons that serve as the denouement to Avery's output. It now becomes most ob-

A 1942 model sheet.

114

"Ed"

#284

A 1942 model sheet alongside this model sheet for 1953's FIELD AND SCREAM illustrates the evolution in drawing styles for Avery's cartoons.

vious how much he had depended on the strength of the sturdy, expensive MGM production level; and without that strength he's like Stan Laurel without Oliver Hardy. His gags are still brilliant, his comic sense is still masterful, and he still appears willing to go just about haywire, but an essential feature of his comic largess seems sorely lacking. The colors are suddenly limited to pale blue and varying shades of gray. Some of the animation is so crude as to compare unfavorably with Farmer Alfalfa. And the four-piece combo that seems to be accompanying Lantz's cartoons certainly invites nostalgia for the stirring strains of the MGM Symphony Orchestra (a luxury allowed only to big-studio cartoon units). It's enough to make the difference between great cartoons and ones that are simply "interesting."

Half of these Lantz cartoons star a pantomimic penguin named Chilly Willy, whom Avery handles as, essentially, Droopy with a tux-

115

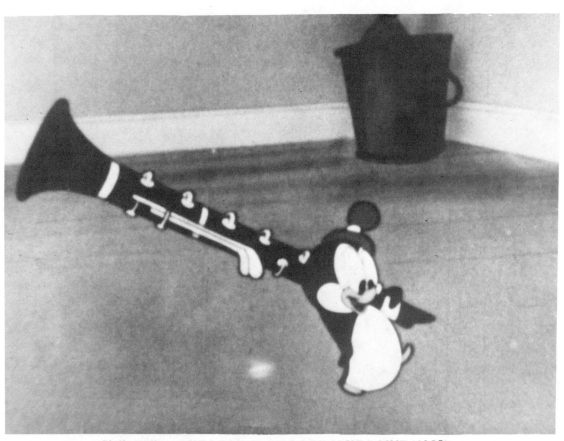

Chilly Willy in THE LEGEND OF ROCKABYE POINT (1955).

THE LEGEND OF ROCKABYE POINT: one eternity.

edo. I'M COLD proves how funny this little nonentity can be, but THE LEGEND OF ROCKABYE POINT, a sterling collaboration between director Tex Avery and story man Michael Maltese, is a frenetic whirlwind of a cartoon, re-working a situation from DEPUTY DROOPY and ROCK-A-BYE BEAR, and sprucing it up with new gags and bright variations on old ones. It involves the frantic interactions of a ravenous polar bear (who runs ahead of his feet), an energetic Chilly Willy (whose feet run ahead of him), and a vicious watchdog (who consists of two unmoving adjacent triangles), over a boatload of fresh fish. Between the resourceful penguin, and his ability to produce clarinets and anvils whenever they seem to be needed, and the ruthless bulldog, and his ability to appear inside of barrels and behind corners and other places where he clearly never went, the bear has an impossible time trying to get any fish for himself—until it occurs to him that the dog would just as soon fall asleep as guard fish, and that a simple chorus of "Rock-a-bye Baby" will suffice to put him out of the way. From there on it's just a kaleidoscope of plots, reactions, attacks, counterattacks, offensives, reprisals, and repeated renditions of this old favorite lullaby, all of them punctuated by varying expressions of anger, alarm, pride, gloom, befuddlement, annoyance, and pleasure that keep registering on the physiognomy of the pliable bulldog. Again, more laughs are prompted by the villain than by the hero, aptly befitting the demonic nature of Avery's humor. By the end of the film, no fish have been nabbed, the penguin has been kicked out of frame, and the two antagonists have become hoary, frosty figures with frothy beards and feeble shivers, and a legend to the seamen of the neighboring waters. And as the bulldog croaks, "Sing it to me again, will ya, Charlie," we see that the old bear has gotten to enjoy his repeated refrains of "Rock-a-bye Baby," which promise to extend for about one eternity.

The most savage and distinct of this bunch is a bizarre little number called SH-H-H-H-H, both written and directed by Avery, and starring an ensemble of UPA-style humans. At the end of the film, a patient with high blood pressure discovers that it's his psychiatrist and his conscientious nurse, who had prescribed peace and quiet for him in the first place, who have been keeping him up all night with their trombone playing and hysterical laughter. The psychiatrist tells him not to get excited about it. The little man stands there, sputters non-verbally, grows crimson in the face, goes "Poof!," and vanishes in a puff of smoke, without a trace. The psychiatrist turns to us and, with some exasperation, complains, "People just won't listen to their doctor's advice!" And with that, he and his nurse go back to their cackling and their trombone playing, as the sound of their callous laughter proceeds past the final credits and on to the end of the reel. A beautiful, caustic note to end a fast and furious career.

A marvel more of content than of form, SH-H-H-H-H illustrates perfectly the dilemma and the demise of a great comic spirit working inside a complicated art. It's worth wondering whether Avery, had he time, might have come up with a style of humor to fit the gangly adolescent oscillation of the post-UPA Lantz style of animation. In the peak that he reached at MGM, his impossible gags refused to stand alone, but accumulated into an impossible universe, where hallucinations assumed the permanence of truths, and truth the shadowy form of hallucination. Dissolving the potency of that universe is like losing one edge of a two-edged sword. In Avery's most dizzying dithyrambs, his animation had the power to make the most farfetched event actually transpire before your very eyes, while his humor had the power to make the weightiest concern vanish in the light of its ridicule—so that all things did and did not exist at the same time, all things were and were not possible, all things were and were not expected, all things were and were not. One of the most extraterrestrial contortions which the limitless medium of film, and its miraculous stepchild animation, have ever been asked to undergo.

A potentially monotonous situation is imbued with all kinds of inventive life in CRAZY MIXED-UP PUP (1954), Avery's first film for Walter Lantz. A man and his dog exchange bloodstreams at the behest of a cockeyed ambulance attendant.

3. THAT WARNER BROTHERS ROWDYISM

Michael Maltese, for years Chuck Jones' chief story man, is probably the greatest comedy writer that ever worked in the cartoon business. His association with Avery is limited to two brief stints, one at Warners in the early forties and the other at the Walter Lantz studios in the mid-fifties; but in this interview, given April 3, 1971, at his home in Hollywood, California, Maltese gives a rounded impression of the working habits in the early Warner Brothers Cartoon Studio. When he went to work for Leon Schlesinger in 1937, Maltese had come to California for the express purpose of being hired by Walt Disney. But somehow this never happened.

MICHAEL MALTESE: My wife and I were walking past the Chinese Theatre, trying our footprints in the cement, and looking at the Pacific Ocean, and finally we were walking back to our apartment in Hollywood when we passed this building at Fernwood and Van Ness, and it said "Looney Tunes and Merrie Melodies." And my wife says, "Hey, I think that's a cartoon studio." I says, "No it isn't, it's a music company. Looney Tunes and Merrie Melodies, it's some kind of crazy music company." And in 1937 who knew too much about Leon Schlesinger? If I had seen any of the cartoons, they didn't register. So she says, "Go in and find out." So I went in and, sure enough, it was a cartoon studio. And I was interviewed and the guy says, "All right, we'll hire you, I'll give you eighteen dollars a week." I says, "I didn't travel clear across country to work for eighteen dollars a week." He says, "Well, how much you want?" I says, "Twenty." So he says, "OK, you're hired as an inbetweener, twenty dollars a week." And I went to work for them, and I went from inbetweening to assistant animating, and I was put in the story department by the front office. They said, "You'd make a good writer." I said, "Naw, naw, I'm testing for animation." They said, "Go in there!"

And when I went in there, in August of 1939, it was more or less like a stenographers' pool. They had two

Michael Maltese, with Jackalope.

story rooms in this beat-up old building which was originally a storehouse for camera equipment and electric lights for the old Warners Studios when they made THE JAZZ SINGER. Jack Miller, Bugs Hardaway, and Tubby Millar were in one room. And down the hall there was another room, and in that room was a crazy bunch—there was Dave Monahan, Rich Hogan, Cal Howard, Tedd Pierce. They were all in one room. I knew they worked there because I'd already been working at the studio for two years, but I never went near them. On my first introduction to them, they were building a bonfire in the middle of the floor like Indians, sitting around with blankets. I looked, and there's these crazy kids. And I was in my twenties myself.

At any rate, when a director, like Tex Avery, or Friz Freleng, or Frank Tashlin, needed a story they'd go into this pool and see who had a story for them. These kids would all bat their heads together and come out with the ideas, and they'd all talk at once, and the directors would jot down notes, and then the guys would draw up sketches and we'd pin up the sketches on these boards on the wall. If, say, the Monahan bunch was being used by Freleng, then Avery was given a story by Hardaway and Miller and Millar. And then when they were through, they in turn would do a picture for Friz, and the other bunch would do one for Avery or Tashlin.

These kids, these cartoon writers, were the backbone of this business. Dave Monahan, Tedd Pierce, Cal Howard, Rich Hogan, Tubby Millar, Jack Miller, and Bugs Hardaway—they're the crazy bunch. They're the ones that came up with the wild humor. With the help of Avery. I'll tell you one thing about Avery, he's a highly sensitive man, he hides it pretty good, and he's got a terrific gag mind. So he'd sit in with these guys.

Then that began to be split up. They took Tubby Millar and put him upstairs. Bugs Hardaway quit in January of forty. Dave Monahan said, "You'll have to excuse me for the day, I'm going to the dentist." And he jumped in his car and headed for the new Max Fleischer Studio in Florida.

But we were not hampered by any front office interference, because Leon Schlesinger had brains enough to keep the hell away and go aboard his yacht. He used to lithp a little bit and he'd say, "I'm goin' on my yachtht." He'd say, 'Whatth cookin', brainth? Anything new in the Thtory Department?" He came back from Mexico once, he had huarachas on, he said, "Whaddaya think of these Mexican cucarachas? Very comfortable

This and the rest of the drawings in this chapter are a few selected animation drawings from a two-second action in LITTLE RED WALKING HOOD, one of Avery's Warner Brothers cartoons (donated by their animator, Irv Spence).

on the feet." He said, "Disney can make the chicken salad, I wanna make chicken shit." He said, "I'll make money."

(At this moment, Tex Avery enters the room.)

AVERY: Remember the cutthroat poker, twenty-five dollars at a dollar a chip?

MALTESE: Yeah! I remember when you gave Leon Schlesinger ten dollars worth of pennies!

AVERY: Boy, he didn't like it. They weren't even rolled, were they?

MALTESE: No! During a poker game, Leon won about ten dollars from Tex, and Tex said, "I'll give it to you after lunch." So he went and got ten dollars worth of pennies, a thousand pennies, and put them in a little brown paper bag, and said, "Here's the ten I owe you, Leon," and he emptied the paper bag and all the pennies went all over the place! He didn't like it.

126

ADAMSON: Why did you do that? Were you angry?
AVERY: No. I thought it would be funny.
MALTESE: It was.
AVERY: But he saw that they weren't rolled, and his secretary had to roll them, and it took about five hours. God!
MALTESE: There's never been a studio like that.
AVERY: It was real loose, and we all had fun. Remember the Coke machine that would let you almost get the next bottle out, but you couldn't? So we took the cap off. . . .
MALTESE: . . . and put in a straw. . . .
AVERY: . . . and we siphoned it. And we sent the mail boy to get a double shot of booze, and poured it in there. . . .
MALTESE: . . . put it in the Cokes. . . .
AVERY: . . . double shot of bourbon. . . .
MALTESE: . . . then we replaced the cap. . . .
AVERY: . . . and found a sucker. It was Art Gobel. Art took that drink, and he went over to the sand pot and spit it right

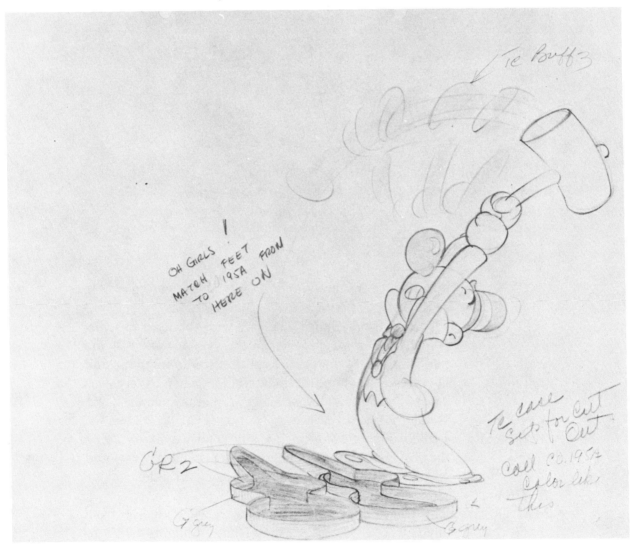

Egghead swings (and the checker passes a note to the inking girls).

out. He felt this hot stream going down, you know. He said, "I've been poisoned!"

MALTESE: I'll tell you one thing: The guy with the most mischievous Bugs Bunny character in the whole studio was the guy sitting right there. He kept that studio jumping, and he invested a spirit in that studio. When Avery was around, you got a kind of gaggy, fun atmosphere.

AVERY: Hell. . . .

MALTESE: Usually anybody working for a director would say, "He's the boss," and there would be problems, but Avery would cheer the guys into this crazy, mixed-up attitude.

AVERY: Hmmmmm.

MALTESE: This you can put down—I don't care what you hear from anybody else—he took Bugs Bunny and instilled into him the character that *made* Bugs Bunny.

AVERY: Aw, Mike . . . I gotta go. . . .

MALTESE: You remember how the guys used to draw caricatures?

And a lot of them were really dirty caricatures of Freleng and Smoky and all those. I had stacks of drawings and caricatures that the guys did. They weren't all dirty, but a lot of them were funny as hell. Tex was a real pixie; he would do a caricature of Friz, see, and he would go off in a corner, and be drawing him, and going, "Heh, heh, heh, heh . . . ," and then he'd look up at Friz and go, "Heh, heh, heh, heh. . . ." Then he'd hand the drawing to him, and go off chuckling, "Mm! Mm! Mm! Mmph!" Just great!

ADAMSON: So you'd sit there at your desk, and this guy's over in a corner doing a drawing of you?

MALTESE: Yeah! And then, to get even, this guy would say, "Haaaah!" and he'd do one. And, first thing you know, it was like a chain reaction—Tedd, myself, Cal, anybody'd be doing it.

AVERY: I recall another gag. I think it was on Tedd Pierce and Freleng—they were in the gag room. And the mail boy

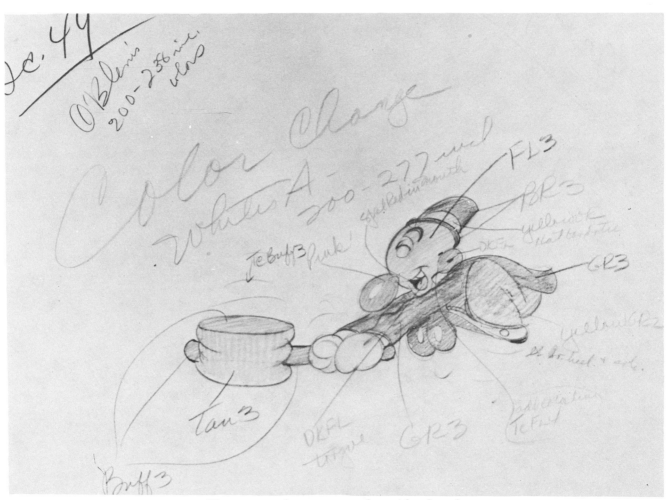

The moment of contact, complete with color scheme.

got some little cardboard thing, and he cut the ends off, went up in the painting and ink room, painted it red like a firecracker, put the fuse in it, and threw it in. And Gee! These guys crawled up the damn wall! And it was the next time that it was a real one. And here the guys just sat there—the thing went KA-POW!

MALTESE: Now, here's the basis for your Bugs Bunny gags.

AVERY: Ha! Ha!

ADAMSON: Sure. . . .

AVERY: Our pranks, in a way, got in the cartoons. Like the fire-cracker. We would work that: a fake, and a fake, and the fuse goes out, and the third one's the real one. Bam!

MALTESE: The day I met Fred Quimby, he says, "I hear you're from Warner Brothers Cartoons." I says, "Yes, Mr. Quimby." He says, "Well, look, if you're going to work with Avery, have this understood: We will not stand for any of that Warner Brothers rowdyism in our cartoons!"

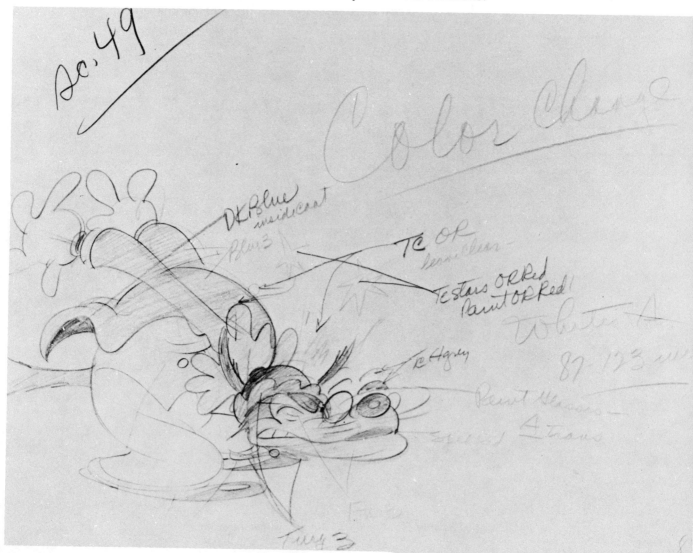

130

AVERY: Heh, heh, heh! We had heard it, too! Well, I gotta go. . . .
MALTESE: The network boys tell us what to make now. About three
            years ago, a big network guy came in from CBS, and he
            said, "I got a great idea for a cartoon series." We said,
            "What?" He said, "A whale. Who's a secret fighter for
            justice. And," he said, "I got the name for it, too. Moby
            Dick!" So Joe Barbera looked at me, and I said, "Get
            him offa me." Here's a whale, you know, and he gets a
            signal—"DA-da-da-DA-da-da-DA! Somebody's in trou-
            ble in Timbuctoo! I must go after it!" And WHSSSH-
            HHHEW! Moby Dick to the rescue!

            So they took Eddie Brandt, a kid who'd written
            some stories, and they stuck him with about fifteen of
            those things. He lost his voice, his nerves. . . .
AVERY: (Genuinely moved) Oh, no.
MALTESE: He lost fifteen pounds, and he got ulcers, doing MOBY

131

DICK. Because all the stuff has to go through the network boys. They weren't even born when we were in this business, thirty or forty years ago, but they look at the stuff and they say, "Well, we don't like this, we don't like that." So Eddie Brandt quit. He started a used furniture place on Lankershim, and he went into selling old comic books, old movie posters, Ken Maynard posters, Johnnie Mack Brown film posters, old stills, and all this stuff, and he is making a fortune! He's got his voice back, he's healthy.

AVERY: And he looks like a whale now!
MALTESE: Yeah, he looks like a whale!
AVERY: I gotta go. . . .
MALTESE: I wanted to ask him, "Who saved you? Moby Dick?"
ADAMSON: I was just down there about an hour ago!
AVERY: Where's that?
ADAMSON: Down at Eddie Brandt's place. I borrowed a poster for

	DOGGONE TIRED to use in the book. You want to buy it? He's selling it for twenty dollars.
AVERY:	Gee! Ow! Oooh!
MALTESE:	When I was there, he asked me did I have any old model sheets or animation drawings.
AVERY:	Of course, the trade rat was Clampett. He saved everything.
MALTESE:	I understand he's got one of the biggest collections in the cartoon business.
AVERY:	You know, we did a bunch of Bugs Bunny commercials on Kool-Aid. I remember I had some old cels and drawings in the back of the car, gotten from camera. So

little kids find out, they say, "Mr. Avery, got any Bugs Bunnies?" So I reach in there, dust them off, and throw them a little batch. WHSSSHHHHEW! Next night, they're waiting for me at the mailbox! "You got any more Bugs Bunnies?" And I said to myself, "Well, if this is gonna be a habit, hell with them." I said, "No, I don't have any more." So then the third time, just one little girl was there. She said, "You got any Bugs Bunnies?" And I said, "Oh, I gave you a whole batch of them!" And she said, 'But my brother takes them to school and sells them for fifty cents apiece!"

(At this moment, Tex Avery leaves the room, as mysteriously as he came.)

MALTESE: Tex is a hard man to work for; he's a perfectionist to this point: that even when he's ready to turn out a good car-

toon, it's still not as good as he wanted to make it. Another director will say, "All right, it came out great. That's fine. I'll take my bows, and next time we'll see what else we can do." I think nobody worried and suffered to make a great cartoon more than Avery did. It was never good enough for him. I told him, "You proved yourself already," but he'd think, "No, it's got to be better!" And he worried himself to the point where it got too difficult for him.

Did you watch him when I tried to flatter him? He goes, "No, no. . . ." It embarrasses him. He'd rather back off than step forward and take justifiable bows.

I had worked on maybe two or three pictures with Avery at Warner Brothers, and when I went to Lantz I didn't know Avery was going to be there. Walter Lantz said, "You know who I'm getting? I'm getting a guy I've been trying to get for years!" "Who?" "Tex Avery!" Because Tex worked with Lantz back in 1929, or whenever, and it was Lantz' ambition to get Tex Avery as his director, for years! He was like a little kid when he told me. "I got Tex Avery—at last!" And it broke his heart when Tex and I quit him.

135

4. TALES OF TAYLOR, TEXAS

Heck Allen became a successful writer of fiction after his twelve-year stretch as Avery's story man at MGM, and now has over thirty Western novels to his credit. Though more absorbed with Western than with animation lore, Allen gives an account which benefits from a novelist's awareness and power of description. This interview was held in all seriousness on April Fool's Day, 1971, at Allen's study, behind his home in California's San Fernando Valley. As the subject sat at his writing desk, under a plaque bearing the motto "My Cup Runneth Amok," he willingly emptied his soul of the affections and grievances he'd acquired during his years in the animation industry. After the many stories I'd heard of writers claiming total authorship for films, it was rather surprising to hear Mr. Allen's opening remarks:

HECK ALLEN: Cartoon-wise, I think you'll find me a pretty thin vein—not much to mine. I was never happy in the business. I was personally happy, because I loved Tex and I loved Rudy Ising, and I think these are great men, but this is a personal thing. I loved to work for them, but I did not like the business, never. Still don't like it. I mean, cartoons don't kill me that dead. I'm sure that Tex, if he leveled with you, probably gave you somewhat the same impression of me: I did my best, but it wasn't really very good.

ADAMSON: He has said you were not much on gags, but very good on the story line.

ALLEN: Nothing at all on gags. There he's being kind, because "not much" is giving me some credit, maybe, "He was something, but not much." No, I was nothing. Period. I used to get, well, they said "laid off," but it was fired, thrown out, regularly, by the downstairs management, because they were well aware of the fact that I wasn't contributing anything except to laugh at Tex's ideas. Weird and wonderful, couldn't help yourself. And then he would periodically re-hire me, it just went like that.

139

Every fall, almost like harvesting the grain, out would go Heck and in would come somebody else for the winter, who wouldn't last. And I'd go home and work on the books, and pretty soon the phone would ring and I'd go back out there and have fun with Tex again.

He got lonely sitting there thinking up all these remarkable ideas, and he liked to have someone to bounce them off. I think my main qualification for the job was that we came from the same cultural background—that is, western, middle-western, south-western types—and he felt at home with me. You know, he's a cowboy at heart, and we could talk together. Actually we had the same kind of sense of humor, although mine was in-turned and his turned outward. In other words, he killed me. I mean, he was the funniest sonofabitch that ever lived. And in turn, I was a good audience for him, and also provided some technical assistance in terms of, oh, dialogue writing, and occasional structural work, which sounds like nothing.

I liked Tex, I thought he was a wonderful fellow, marvelous to work with, and before him my years in the business were spent with Rudy Ising, another marvelous fellow. Although I don't know Chuck Jones, I know he does remarkable stuff. I think that Chuck and Tex are simply geniuses, but it's a genius in a field that's always been foreign to me. If I was able to provide anything, it was simply because I was bright enough. I might have been of the same help to somebody making educational shorts or travelogues, just because if you have a mind, you can help in any intellectual situation simply by being there. I came up with an occasional idea, you know, the percentage of accident permits you to do that. But I would say that Tex had to provide ninety-eight percent of everything that went into those cartoons. And his influence pervaded and permeated the product far beyond the story room.

ADAMSON: Then you seem to feel, in reference to Avery's remark, that you didn't even contribute that much as far as story was concerned.

ALLEN: No, I didn't. It's kind of him, and typical of him. I think, quite literally, that Tex would honestly believe that I was of more help to him than I was. His position, as always, is real. If I see those cartoons today, I'll sit there and laugh, oh shit, I can remember the situation and how it came up and how we worked on it, but it's all Tex's stuff.

Tex, of course, was always totally in charge of anything he ever did. That's why, to this day, he works alone; he just doesn't want to argue with people. And

140

I never argued with him. Well, how could you? I mean, you're sitting there knocked out on your chair, laughing your ass off all day long, you can't very well argue with the guy that's bringing the tears to your eyes. With Tex and I it was just like two men who enjoyed each other in a sort of old-fashioned male way which wouldn't be understood today. I thought, and think, that he's a genuine, native, American genius.

ADAMSON: You say you came from similar backgrounds. . . .

ALLEN: I was born and raised in Jackson County, Missouri; he was born and raised in Taylor, Texas. When we were growing up in our particular home towns, they were rural, and the type of things that's treated nostalgically today in literature by writers like MacKinlay Kantor, who write of the small-town America. It really existed at one time. Anyone your age wouldn't believe it, they'd have to see pictures. We'd sit there all day long and amuse each other with tales of Taylor, Texas, or Jackson or Clay County, Missouri. We were old boys, and I think it had a great deal to do with getting along.

Rich Hogan, the story man Tex had when he came over to MGM from Warner Brothers, was Tex's audience over there. Rich was drafted, and I did not get a proper chance to rate him as a gagman. Whether he was more help to Tex than I was, I cannot say. As a matter of personal experience with Tex, though, I would have to doubt it.

I think, really, to anyone trying to understand Tex Avery, trying to do something publishable about him, that's the main point—that he has done it all alone. He never had any help, as I see it.

Now Chuck Jones, I don't care how brilliant Chuck is (and I have heard enough times that he is brilliant), he didn't do it all by himself. He had in this Mike Maltese an extremely able gagman and a good story man, so he had help.

Tex never had anybody. He laid the pictures out for the goddam background man; he did everything for the so-called character man, who draws the models of the character. Tex did it all, the guy just cleaned up after him. And that's really what I was doing, cleaning up after him. Like if we had three pages of dialogue, he would scratch it out with his lead pencil, and I'd take this stuff and translate it into English, you know,

Avery provided the guffaws for these characters in his Warner Brothers cartoons.
THE PENGUIN PARADE (1938).

and type it up. Big deal. Anybody could have done it. But he did everything, including some of the voices. If talent weren't available, hell, he'd go and do the voice himself. So he's really the original one-man band.

ADAMSON: Do you remember which voices he did?

ALLEN: Oh, he did Droopy a lot of times. He didn't customarily do the character, Bill Thompson did it; but occasionally when Thompson wouldn't show up, or we had to have a line or something, hell, Tex'd just go record it. Couldn't tell the difference.**

Tex was a bearcat for dialogue. God, he would have twenty or thirty takes on a line, and to me, then

---

** Only upon questioning did Avery admit that he is the voice for Junior, of George and Junior, and the very similar voice of Willoughby, the hunting dog in THE HECKLING HARE, THE CRACKPOT QUAIL, and OF FOX AND HOUNDS. At Warners, his voice pops up from time to time embodied in a hippo or a walrus who laughs so hard he can hardly take his next breath. Avery also does the chuckle of the bulldog in BAD LUCK BLACKIE. For anyone who wants a clue to what Avery's real voice sounds like, there are the little ouches that come out of a bottle in DEPUTY DROOPY.—JA3.

or now, it didn't make that much difference. We would sit in that projection room and run those goddam things over and over and over and over and over again. Hell, I couldn't tell one from the other. But Tex would eventually pick one, and I'd say, "Yeah! Just the one!"

Tex still comes out here occasionally and drops in and we chat for an hour. He was born in a small town called Taylor, Texas, which is in mid-Texas, and came out here as a boy. His hobby is racing pigeons. He loves animals; his daughter is genuine zoophile. Tex, I think, is a loner, right down to his last gasp; and I doubt very much if his family knows him. Do you follow me? He's extremely devoted to his family. He must be a marvelous father, because he has no small bone in his body. He's a completely generous man, a warm man, he's enthusiastic and he likes people, he is very sensitive, really. And, after all these years, I don't know a hell of a lot about Tex. It's an emotional relationship we've had.

Tex, by the way, is a lineal blood descendant of

HAMATEUR NIGHT (1938).

143

Judge Roy Bean. Did you ever hear of the "Law West of the Pecos"? Well, Roy Bean was a cantankerous old drunk who set himself up out on the Pecos River in this little goddam town which he invented called Langtry, Texas. Now, Langtry he named after Lily Langtry, who was the reigning stage beauty and singer of her day. And this old goat, sitting way out on the Pecos River in Comanche land, then, had a big crush on this broad sitting in New York. And he named his goddamned saloon after her—The Jersey Lily. He had the post office there, and announced himself to be the Justice of the Peace for the whole area of Texas west of the Pecos—and he was. And he is the author of that famed cliché about one highwayman who was brought in there, really a man of no great crime at all, but Judge Bean told him very calmly that he would be given a fair trial and then hung. And this was the way he dispensed his justice. And he was a very funny man. I mean, he had an outrageous sense of humor, he would go ahead and hang some of these guys. I can see he even looks like Tex. If you pull away the beard and the long hair of the time, you'd say, "Jesus Christ, that could be Tex's uncle, no two ways about it."*So he is a true, old time Texas boy. I think this, very much, gives flavor to his humor. Tex's middle name is Bean, and it comes from the family of Judge Roy Bean. His name is Fred Bean Avery.

ADAMSON: Gee. No wonder people call him Tex.

ALLEN: He's just about as "Tex" as you can get. His stuff, and the style he's set (which I am convinced he set, and Jones and Freleng just followed) is earthy. This stuff that they're still doing with that damn coyote and the roadrunner, this is fundamental Tex Avery stuff.

I think Chuck Jones was kind of a split personality in that business. He was an intellectual in a nonintellectual business. Now, I don't know that Tex or Fritz are not intellectuals, but I don't think that either one would be called an intellectual. And being an intellectual is a helluva handicap, in almost anything. It's always been a handicap to me. I regard myself as an intellectual; more importantly, other people regard me as an intellectual, so that's what I'm stuck with. "Yeah, he's funny,

* Avery is indeed related to Roy Bean (1828–1903), a long-standing Texas legend. Roy Bean's real name was Roy Boone, and he was descended from Daniel Boone. Will it never end?—JA3.

but y'know, he went to school." And these people who built the cartoon empire, as you well know, are not very often found with higher educational backgrounds. These are men that came right out of high school, they had to work and they did, and they were artistically inclined and they gathered out here. So, if you were educated, either self- or officially, well, in that business you're an intellectual and you don't really belong.

I hated the business, really, and only because I wasn't meant to be in it. I knew it and it killed me. I started writing books only after ten or twelve years in that damn Mickey Mouse Factory, and had I gone into the books right off the bat I probably would be independently wealthy today. Probably, hell! I would be.

ADAMSON: When did you start there?

ALLEN: By God, I don't know. I went to college for two and a half years, and then dropped out. I had an older brother out here who was an animator with Harman-Ising, and he said, "If you're not happy in school, come out and go to work." Which I did. I started out here in the original MGM cartoon unit, which consisted of Joe Barbera, Bill Hanna, C. G. Maxwell, Fred MacAlpine, my brother Bob Allen, and myself, and a couple of New Yorkers—Mike Meyers and Dan Gordon. That was it. In 1937, I believe. and I finally began to get out of MGM in 1950 when my first novel came out. It was successful, and showed me that I didn't have to work for a living. I was at MGM off and on after that, but never under contract.

ADAMSON: What was your first novel called?

ALLEN: Called *No Survivors*. It was a Custer exposé. The first one; there've been a hundred of them since, making a real schmuck out of Custer. Now it's the popular thing to do with every hero.

ADAMSON: It didn't take you very long to get established, then.

ALLEN: No. Immediately. It was just pure luck. The book was quite successful; it's still in print, twenty years later. So I had a wonderful time for those years, but for the life of me I can't remember what the hell I was doing that was so much fun. They had cute girls. I wasn't married for a while, and swung pretty good. It was like being a wolf in a sheep pen, you know. I just couldn't believe it, coming from Jackson County. So that was one reason I didn't get much done.

ADAMSON: Where did you get this name of yours, this "Heck" business?

ALLEN: I don't know, it's a child's name. When I quit the cartoons, I just sort of left it with them. Psychologically,

145

The competition: Bill Hanna and Joe Barbera's Tom & Jerry.

	I wanted a complete break. As I look back, the dropping of the name was deliberate, it wasn't accidental.
ADAMSON:	What was the atmosphere like around the MGM animation department?
ALLEN:	Well, it was great. After Bill and Joe got their Tom and Jerry series launched, there was a very competitive feeling between them and Tex. Very competitive. And Tex always felt, and I think he was correct, that Bill and Joe were the darlings of Fred Quimby's eye. And that favoritism rankled quite a bit. Fred Quimby was the wrong man of all time to be in charge of a laugh factory. But he did know, because somebody *told* him, that those Tom and Jerrys were pretty damn funny, and he stuck with that idea, and he was faithful to it. Fortunately for him, it was good business.

However, I must admit of some prejudice in the case of Fred Quimby, because he was the instrument of throwing me out of there periodically. We didn't get along at all. I think it might have had something to do with the fact that I would periodically tell him he didn't know anything about animated cartoons. In later years, when he retired, and I saw him a couple of times over in Beverly Hills, he was the soul of graciousness to me, acted as though we had been in love all those years out there. And we weren't. He very actively disliked me, because I was a "troublemaker." And I was fired at least seven or eight times in twelve years. But for most of the people out there, I think it was a pretty happy ship, because most of them belonged there.

ADAMSON:	They enjoyed animation.
ALLEN:	That's it. And most of them are still in it.
ADAMSON:	Was Quimby a guy who didn't understand cartoons, or just didn't understand anything?
ALLEN:	I don't think he understood cartoons at all. I don't think that you can become a senior vice-president of a large corporation and be stupid. I think that in his cold, Hibernian way, he was very, very good at what he needed to do to survive in the corporate structure as a vice-president. What that was, I still don't know, but I'm sure that Fred C. was very, very good at it. Hugh Harman and Rudy Ising were dear, sweet men. Neither one of them had the right animal qualifications for survival in the Hollywood jungle. And they didn't survive. Fred Quimby, on the other hand, had no qualification whatever artistically, even to sit in judgment. Yet he survived. Demonstrating the problem that is still extant with the motion picture business: non-talent controlling talent. Fred Quimby was a stereotype. There's

Fred Quimby.

nothing personal in what I say about Fred Quimby. And this is still the problem, these ungifted people in charge of extremely sensitive art forms. The wonder is that anything gets through. The wonder is that a Tex Avery can come through to the screen at all. Or a Chuck Jones, or Friz Freleng, or any of them.

MGM was an ant-heap of industry and activity at that time—just swarming with picture-shooting all over the three lots they had then. We were out on "Lot 2" there. My God! I used to spend half my time out there on some set watching them make motion pictures. You'd just sneak out, climb out on the back roof, go over the edge, drop to the ground—like Apaches or Comanches going over the stockade wall—and go watch them make real pictures. The only reason I got away with it was that Tex was extremely interested in the same thing. He has been, all his life, a frustrated live-action director, and he would have been an absolutely great one.

Tex never understood the quality and extent of his own genius. Otherwise he would have simply picked up his briefcase, gone up on the front lot, and said, "I'm Tex Avery. I can make the funniest goddam live-action pictures you ever saw in your life, and we'll get rich together." But he never did. He is totally modest—another great factor. He doesn't understand to this day that he's been a force in the animated cartoon business. It's kind of nice to know a man who is genuinely modest—and he's genuinely modest. It's not a pose, which is easy to strike, the old "Oh shucks, I didn't do nuthin'." That's not the way he is at all. But he is intent upon every facet of entertainment. Tex loves to be funny; I think he'd kill himself to get a laugh. And this is not in the public sense. He doesn't show off in public, he's very quiet. This is to provide a laugh for somebody in a theater 2000 miles and two years away from right then. His whole life is humor. If he were able to write, or inspired in that direction, I think he'd do a best-selling novel. But he's oriented toward what he's doing.

And we talked about it. My God, we'd sit there and concoct a Red Skelton Western, and in an afternoon we'd have the whole damn thing—premise, jokes, line continuity—and nothing came of it. Not a thing. I don't think he ever even talked to Skelton. Tex was the kind of a guy who would be watching the Pete Smith shorts being made, and he would just get to biting his nails, and he'd go over to the director, and he'd say, "Hey, why don't you have that guy do this and that. . . ." And the guy would just crack up. Tex would stand there and give those guys five hundred dollars worth of jokes in a minute. Unbelievable. The most unbelievable thing was that they didn't appreciate it, that they didn't snare him and elevate him to the papacy of humor on the front lot. Tex could have been a Frank Capra or whatever at this business, could have gone completely to the top. The cartoon business is full of brilliant people like that who never get heard of. Their tragic flaw is that they're hung up on these goddam little figures running around on that drawing board. See? They've been infected with that. Literally, the animation bug is in the blood.

ADAMSON: Yeah, always, the movement of drawings.

ALLEN: If he were working today, I see Tex doing a thing on integration—you know, with a black cat and a white cat and the relationship between them. And he'd have the liberals and the squares rolling on the floor together! And not understanding how they got there! And the guy who would least understand . . . is Tex.

5. YOU COULDN'T GET CHAPLIN IN A MILK BOTTLE

Avery (Anglo-Saxon): deriv. of Aelfric; definition: king of the elves.

Among the initiates, Tex Avery has reputation enough to rank with Pecos Bill. Walter Lantz explains that, "The thing about Avery is that he can write a cartoon, lay it out, time it, do the whole thing himself. And when he's finished, it's great. He just knows comedy." "Tex is great, I learned a lot from him," Chuck Jones tells us, and another Warner colleague, Friz Freleng, attests, "He had a very good sense of humor, on or off the animation board." "Tex was a great story man and a great gag man. He's even funnier than his pictures," says Bob Clampett—a dizzying prospect. "I like anything Tex Avery ever did," and "Tex Avery, he's a master," pour forth endlessly from old animators, long-standing Disney men, animation instructors in universities, anybody who knows the business well, whether or not you happened to have asked them what their opinion was. Once, standing in the halls at Cascade Studios, where Avery now works, I was accosted by one of his co-workers, who insisted, "This guy's a legend! That's what you gotta capture about him! The legend!"

Avery adheres to the John Ford policy in recalling his career, preferring the recounting of anecdotes and the re-telling of favorite gags to any form of pontification on the nature of his art. Casual, slow, relaxed, and amiable, like some character out of a Chuck Jones cartoon, Avery gives off the gracious aura of a man without an ounce of hatred or malice in his entire being. As he recounts his bygone binges of destruction, one senses a grandfatherly joy at having been able to bring off so much violence in his time without once having to hurt anybody. Even when discussing ancient grievances, he gives ample evidence of his power to make a joke out of anything. This interview is an amalgamated version of three separate sessions held in conference rooms and in Avery's office at Cascade Studios, on June 19, 1969; November 13, 1969; and March 25, 1971.

ADAMSON: What art training have you had?
AVERY: Oh, I was on the high school annual, that cartoon bit. The only guy there who could handle a pencil. Who could hold one. I'd illustrate the annuals, and we had

Tex Avery

a monthly magazine. And I took a little three-month summer course up in Chicago, at the Chicago Art Institute. I enjoyed that. We had everything; we had life drawing, still, color, composition. And our cartoon courses were at night. The newspaper cartoonists would come over, from the *Chicago Tribune* and so forth. We had the best of cartoonists there. Not teachers. Men who had made it. McKutcheon, Schumaker—met quite a few of the guys. And I still retain some of their originals, some of the old strips. They might be valuable.

ADAMSON: How did you get into animation?

AVERY: Well, gosh, when I finished high school I drove some people out for a six-week deal, and I liked it out here and I decided to stay. I kept working nights on a cartoon strip. Boy, I sent it everywhere. I didn't get anything but rejects. But animation to me was nothing, it was just a step I had to go through till I got my strip going. I met a fella who knew a girl who was head of the inking and painting at Walter Lantz's, so I inked and painted for a while. (They had guys that inked then; now it's just girls.) Then I worked up into inbetweens, then about that time Disney raided the whole West Coast for talent. And the three-quarters of us who were left knew nothing of animation. We had just been inbetweening.

ADAMSON: What happened to the strip, then?

AVERY: Gave it up! For the longest time I just had no interest in animation. I was still thinking, "Sure, I'll try this, but I'll still stick to my strip." But I kept on getting nothing but rejects, so I said, "Well, I'm going to try animation. This is the coming thing." And then I really worked hard at it. Soon as I hit Warners, boy, I'd stay up nights!

And I never was too great an artist. I realized there at Lantz's that most of these fellows could draw rings around me. I could put it over crudely, and that was enough to get by at the time, but a lot of these guys, your top Disney men, as far as anatomy or whatnot—hell, you can't touch 'em! Out of that batch that I worked with was Preston Blair, who turned out to be a top Disney man, Les Kline, who's still in animation, and several other big animators. I thought, Brother! Why fight it? I'll never make it! Go the other route! And I'm glad I did. My goodness, I've enjoyed that a lot more than I would have enjoyed just animating scenes all my life.

ADAMSON: Do animators all wish they were directors?

AVERY: Not necessarily, no. Some wouldn't accept it if you

155

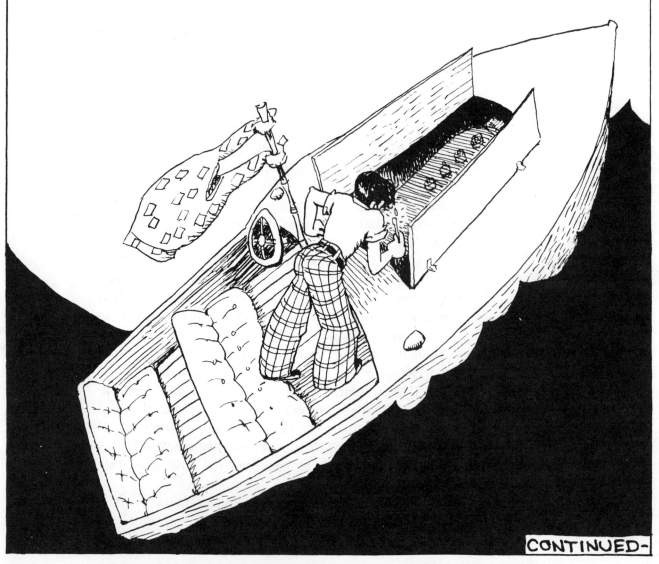

Once a week these one-panel adventures were posted by Avery on a high school bulletin board, and gawkers jammed traffic in the halls.

gave it to them. Others that think they've got it, they haven't got it. No, they're content. Especially the good ones, because they can take something that's very mediocre and make something good out of it. They get new scenes all the time, but it's a monotonous thing, in a way. I couldn't do that for twenty-five years. I'd get tired of it. But I never got tired of directing cartoons. It was always a new challenge.

Recently somebody ran me the Lantz cartoon with the first scene I ever animated. I thought, "I'll never recognize it." And as soon as the scene came on, I remembered it! Gee whiz, what a lousy scene! Just a big bunch of nothing!

They gave me a scene to animate once: Oswald was on board ship with some guy with a peg leg, and I was supposed to show this guy firing a cannon. Well, I had the cannon droop and the ball roll out, then the cannon pointed straight up, then he went to light the fuse and it went out. I built it up from ten feet to sixty feet. The drawings kept stacking up! He jammed the cannonball into the cannon with his peg leg, and then walked around to the back with the cannonball on his leg, then he threw the ball into the cannon and the peg leg went in too. When he finally got it all organized, then the fuse went out. I don't know, it just went on and on.

We had no footage limit, and Walt said, "Heck, yeah, we'll leave it in." Later on, at Metro, I had to time *everything* out. We had a limit: six hundred feet, without titles. One foot over that, for three hundred prints, at Technicolor prices, was too much, and the studio would complain. "You're giving that footage away to the theaters!" Once in a while, an animator would come and say, "I just can't do it in that time— give me another foot!" Then I'd say, "All right, we'll cut somewhere else."

While I was at Lantz's, in the early thirties, an incident occurred that made me feel the animation business owed me a living. We were all a group of crazy gagsters that would attempt anything for a laugh, and one routine was the rubber band and paper spitball shot at the back of the head. You'd pop a guy, hit him, and he'd yell, "Bull's-eye!" We had one goof there that had actually been kicked in the head by a horse! (Had a huge scar across his forehead.) He was really a bit off. He went a step further and used a wire paper clip. One of the boys yelled, "Look out, Tex!" and I turned and caught the clip in my left eye. That lost me one eye in a split second.*

Bill Nolan, who was Lantz's partner, had a crew, and Walter Lantz had another crew; there were two crews. I'd sell Bill a few gags once in a while, and he said, "Why don't you do a story?" I wrote two, and he said, "Go ahead, do them."

The Termite Terrace Crew in 1935, as preserved for all time in Bob Clampett's home movies. From left to right: Virgil Ross, Sid Sutherland, Tex Avery, Chuck Jones, Bob Clampett (courtesy of Bob Clampett).

* As this story indicates, Avery has been blind in one eye since his early twenties. This would seem to be a serious handicap to an animator, but there are many occasions when a character's apparent weightlessness or two-dimensionality is made to add to the comic effect.—JA3.

Frederick Avery

Avery's pre-animation calling card.

Avery demonstrates a take for an animator (courtesy of Bob Clampett).

But the exposure sheets in those days were nothing, you could just say, "Well, a fellow goes over here and he lights a candle, gets a drink of water, and stumbles over the cat. Let's see, it would take da-da-da, over there, back here . . ." and you'd tear off a bunch of exposure sheets and do it in about twenty feet and give it to an animator. But it was that loose; you didn't know whether you were going to have a thousand-foot picture or a five-hundred-foot picture.

ADAMSON: On the basis of that, you were a director?

AVERY: That's right. That's what I called myself. I was having money trouble at Lantz's. Then I heard there was going to be a change over at Warners, and I applied, I said I'd directed two cartoons. Looking back, I don't know why or how Schlesinger gambled on me. Evidently he was quite desperate. He had a fellow by the name of Tom Palmer, I think, and he wasn't satisfied. He said, "I'll try you. I'll try you on one picture. I've got some boys here—they're not renegades, but they don't get along with the other two crews. They're not satisfied working with the people they're working with." Evidently there was some rub. And he gave me Chuck Jones, Bob Clampett, and Bob Cannon. Chuck was creative; so was Bob Clampett. Bob Cannon was a terrific draftsman. And they were tickled to death; they wanted to get a "new group" going, and "we could do it," and "let's make some funny pictures." It was very encouraging, and a wonderful thing to step into, since I had so much enthusiasm in the people and they were on my side. Most of the time, you go into a new studio and, boy, they start cutting you up!

We worked every night—Jones, Clampett, and I were all young and full of ambition. My gosh, nothing stopped us! We encouraged each other, and we really had a good ball rolling. I guess Schlesinger saw the light; he said, "Well, I'll take you boys away from the main plant." He put us up in our own little shack over on the Sunset lot, completely separated from the Schlesinger Studio, in some old dressing room or toilet or something, a little cottage sort of thing. We called it Termite Terrace. And he was smart; he didn't disturb us. We were all alone out there, and he knew nothing of what went on.

We started going through the old cartoons that had been made and we came across one of Friz Freleng's. He had a cartoon, I think it was called I HAVEN'T GOT A HAT, and he had these little guys coming up on a stage and doing different acts, and then here comes

160

CHUCK JONES—BOB CLAMPETT & TEX AVERY DRAWN by TEX AVERY.

Jones, Clampett, and Avery, by Avery. In a post-RURAL RIDING HOOD historical perspective, it's surprising to find out that when Chuck Jones wanted to draw a cow with udders on, and Bob Clampett wanted to reduce a fan dancer to barest essentials, Tex Avery of all people remained fastidiously opposed. It's also surprising to find a man so effectively satirizing himself. (courtesy of Bob Clampett).

a big hog and he stutters, trying to recite a poem. He stutters, and it's funny as heck. On the basis of that, we said, "Let's try a pig." We talked Schlesinger into it, and we designed Porky Pig. So, we started on those, and they got over, as good as anything, that was around. Freleng was making color pictures; he was the Number One Boy. Then we were allowed to make color pictures, which we were tickled with. After that, since I'm quite a duck hunter, we started kicking around a duck picture. What eventually came out of that was Daffy Duck.

Eventually it all spread out: Chuck Jones and Bob Clampett branched out on their own and took their own crews. Then Clampett got out of cartoons and went

161

into early television doing puppets with Stan Freberg.

ADAMSON: How did Bugs Bunny come into being?

AVERY: Oh, we wanted a rabbit, so we thought of a Brooklyn-ese smartaleck who knew everything—nothing bothered him. Of course, the voice meant everything. We needed a human foil to work with him, so we had a little chubby guy to be outwitted by the smartaleck rabbit, and in the same cartoon Elmer Fudd was born. We didn't feel that we had anything until we got it on the screen and it got quite a few laughs. After we ran it and previewed it and so forth, Warners liked it and the exhibitors liked it, and so of course Leon Schlesinger ran down and said, "Boy, give us as many of those as you can!" Which we did.

When Schlesinger died, he was credited with having created Bugs Bunny. And of course all the other directors jumped up and said no, I did it, I did it, I did it. They started searching back through their old cartoons thinking, "Wait a minute, didn't I do a picture with a rabbit in it?" If anyone views A WILD HARE they will find the personality that I gave the rabbit has not changed over the years. So, after the poor old boy died, why, I think I was finally given credit for creating Bugs Bunny by Edward Selzer, the new producer.

All characters develop, of course. You take your Woody Woodpecker, your Donald Duck; the first ones were crude, awful-looking things. The same way with the rabbit. He wasn't pleasant, but we kept refining him until we had a good-looking rabbit. But that all came about through one cartoon after another—evolution. I think voices have an awful lot to do with the success of a cartoon character. Going back to Donald Duck: they had the guy that could do that crazy duck voice, and they built a character around it. The voice came before the duck. The guy said, "I can talk like a duck," and they said, "Gee, man, that's funny!" And of course going clear back to the old Popeye—the husky voice. And Droopy had a definite voice.

But I've always felt that what you did with a character was even more important than the character itself. Bugs Bunny could have been a bird. Donald Duck could have been any character that blew its top every ten feet. It isn't what you see on the screen, it's what they say and do that builds up their personality. As a drawing, Bugs Bunny has an awful lot in common with Max Hare from THE TORTOISE AND THE HARE, one of Walt Disney's old Silly Symphonies. Mr. Disney was polite enough never to mention it, because he didn't

Max Hare in Walt Disney's THE TORTOISE AND THE HARE (1934).

Bugs Bunny in Tex Avery's THE HECKLING HARE (1941).

have to. People had been copying him for years, his bears and everything else, but he never did complain. He evidently looked at us as parasites. But if you look back, why, my goodness, there's a rabbit that looked a heck of a lot like Bugs Bunny, as far as the drawing goes. But he wasn't Bugs Bunny without the gags that we gave him.

ADAMSON: Where did "What's up, Doc?" come from?

AVERY: I was fresh from Texas when I came out here, I came out in twenty-eight or twenty-nine. At that time, down there you called everyone "Doc," it was a high school bit. "Hey, Doc! Whaddya know!" "What's up, Doc?" "How ya been today, Doc?" Everything was Doc! And I came out here, and I met a few guys, and they said, "Where do you get that Doc stuff?" Well, it was just an expression. I don't know how far it spread, maybe it didn't leave Dallas, Texas.

So when we hit on the rabbit, we decided he was going to be a smartaleck rabbit, but casual about it, and I think the opening line in the very first one was "Eh, what's up, Doc?" And, gee, it floored 'em! They expected the rabbit to scream, or anything but make a casual remark—here's a guy with a gun in his face! It got such a laugh that we said, "Boy, we'll do that every chance we get." It became a series of "What's up Docs."

ADAMSON: Did it always get a laugh?

AVERY: Oh, well, most of the time. I guess we overdid it eventually.

Frank Tashlin was working for Schlesinger then, too. We called him Tish-Tash. He had a cartoon strip, and he fooled around. He would see cartoons and he would go to the old slapstick movies with a little flashlight and a little black notebook, and he would note down every Charlie Chaplin and every Laurel and Hardy gag he saw. We used to kid him about his little black book, because he was always looking in it for a joke. Well, the laugh was on us. He went much further in this gag business than we ever did.

He finally did a cartoon that Schlesinger didn't like and Schlesinger jumped on him for it. Tashlin was a temperamental person, so he said, "Heck with it, I'll pull out." That guy, he went up and up! He wrote the Bob Hope picture, PALEFACE, and he directed SON OF PALEFACE, and several other good pictures. But he did what we had always wanted to do. So many times we had told ourselves, "My gosh, this gag may be funny animated, but if it were only in live action, it would be terrific!" What Tash did was to take the old clichés of the cartoon gags and act them out live. And that made him a name! And they were real funny pictures.

When I was at Warners, we did a takeoff on the Fitzpatrick travelogues. We had spot gags with a running gag and we called it THE ISLE OF PINGO PONGO. In other words, we had a group of jokes, and we had to tag it, we couldn't just end with a joke, so we had the running gag of the little fellow coming in as the narrator to start another scene. The little fellow would come in with a violin case and he'd say, "Now Boss?" And the narrator would say, "No, not now. Sorry!" And throughout the picture, why, the little fellow would come back and say, "Now Boss?" The man says, "No."

Of course, remember this is a takeoff on the old Fitzpatrick travelogues. In those days, they were the only travelogues made. And Metro had them for years. And they always ended with a sunset. "And as the sun sinks slowly in the west, we bid you farewell. . . ." Regardless of where he was: India, China. He'd find a sunset every time!

So when we get to the end of our picture, we had the glorious sunset shot with the sun sinking and, a la Fitzpatrick, the narrator says, "And now, we leave you as the sun sinks slowly in the west. As the sun sinks slowly in the west." The sun stays there. Finally the little fellow comes in, with his violin case. He says, "Now Boss?" And the man says, "Yes, now." He opens the violin case and takes out a rifle and he shoots the sun. And the sun drops. And the man says, "Goodnight!"

They were mostly dialogue gags, and we used animals a lot. And I thought it would be so much better if they were live animals. So I kicked it around and found out that I could double expose cartoon mouths over live animals. I made a test for myself, on my own, and I presented it to Schlesinger and I gave him a script, and he said, "Well, you take it over to the head of shorts at Warners," a fellow by the name of Hollingshead. I showed it to him and he loved it. He said, "Sure we'll make one. Make a pilot." So then I went back to Schlesinger saying what Hollingshead told me, but Schlesinger wanted his cartoons. I said, "Well, I'll make a pilot over the weekends. Get a camera and we'll shoot the zoos and animals." Well, he said, "No, I'll pay you for your scripts and your gags, and we'll let Warners

165

'DAFFY DUCK AND EGGHEAD'

A
MERRIE MELODIE CARTOON
IN TECHNICOLOR
A LEON SCHLESINGER
Production

do the films, because we're in the business of making cartoons." So we had quite an argument there and it eventually ended up with him laying me off for an eight-week period. Meanwhile, he told me I could do anything I wanted to with the idea, but he didn't want to have anything to do with it.

I had two old friends that I had met at Universal, Bob Carlysle and Jerry Fairbanks; they were making "Odd Occupations" for Paramount. So I went to Bob and showed him my idea, and we got an animal, a little stock shot of a desert horn toad from the library, and I animated one line: "I don't care what you say, I'm horny." We shot it. We sent a script back to Paramount and they went for it immediately. So I made three there; I had a deal with the boys, and there again I felt that I was entitled to a little more money. We had a falling out and I sold out my portion to Fairbanks. Later, I was sorry that it didn't work out better for me financially, because those things ran six or seven years and were very successful, and won at least one Oscar. [Note: The series was called SPEAKING OF ANIMALS. See FILMOGRAPHY.]

ADAMSON: What was Schlesinger like to work for?

AVERY: He was a good boss. Though hard to get money out of. He didn't know what you were making till he saw it on film. He might say, "What are you doing?" and we'd say, "Well, we're making a Western with Bugs Bunny," or whatever, and he'd say, "Fine." Then he wouldn't know anything more about it until the rough cut. Then he'd say, "Gee, that's great! Give me another one just like it! That's wonderful!" Or if he didn't like it, he'd say, "Don't give me one like that any more. I don't like it." And, as a result, we all had so much liberty over there, and I think it showed in our cartoons. Nothing was held back; we had hardly any censorship, and no problems.

He loved to gamble. We got paid on a Thursday; we'd get our checks at noon, and we'd cash 'em. There were about five of us—Bob McKimson, Friz Freleng, Tex Avery, Henry Bender, Ray Katz. At 5:00 every Thursday we'd get a call: "Mr. Schlesinger's office, please." We'd go in there, and he's got twenty-five little poker chips stacked up. You put down twenty-five dollars. You couldn't buy any more chips. It's cutthroat poker at a dollar a chip: You lose your twenty-five dollars and you go home. Someone would win $125 every week. But that was our boss! You had to go in there whether you wanted to or not! Here we were in this lush office, and there were times when he'd say, "Fellas, can't I buy in? I'll give you two dollars a chip." We'd say, "No, Chief. Sorry. Good night." And out he'd walk.

I wanted a kick in salary once; I think it was a twenty-five-dollar raise. And I was supposed to wait another six months for it. He said, "Well, Tex, what I'll do, I'll get the cards out. I'll cut you high card, for fifty dollars or nothing. If you lose, you won't get another dime for a year." I'll never forget, he had an eight and I had a jack. So he pushed a button, called the girl in, and said, "OK, tear it up and put another fifty dollars on him." People won't believe that, unless they knew Schlesinger.

After he retired, his right-hand man, a fellow by the name of Henry Bender, would take him out to the track every day, to gamble. But to get a dollar out of him, boy!

Then you get over to Metro, and things were different. You had to fight for what you thought was right. Fred Quimby was strictly a businessman, he knew nothing about stories or gags or whatnot, and he'd ad-

167

Avery patiently attempting to explain a storyboard to Fred Quimby.

mit it. There were some things that we felt would make good cartoons, and he would knock 'em over. We'd have the storyboard all set up, and we'd show it to him and explain everything, and he'd look at it and say, "Why does he do this?" Then we'd have to go back and explain it to him again and point out all the jokes, and he'd just stand there and look at it. Then he'd shake his head; then he'd look at it some more; then he'd walk all the way around the room and come back to us and say, "Boys . . . I don't like it."

Of course, he was between two fires. We got smart, and we would wait until it got close to our deadline and we'd say, "Chief, this is all we've got! The only way to keep from making this show is to lay the animators off. This is all we've got!" So we got by with some things. That's how we did SYMPHONY IN SLANG, where we illustrated literally a lot of popular expressions—"I was in a pickle," "I went to pieces." He had a hell of a time trying to understand that one.

WHAT'S BUZZIN' BUZZARD (1943).

The cartoon he really hated was WHAT'S BUZZIN'
BUZZARD, about two buzzards trying to devour each
other. He darn near threw up every time he saw it.
Finally we got a notice that "This film has been chosen
to be preserved in the Library of Congress Film Collection." He said, "Aw, they coulda picked a better one
than that."

He was really impossible. Goodness! Boy! Damn!
Schlesinger had a sense of humor—if he saw something
funny he'd laugh. But Quimby, you couldn't get him
to laugh. Poor old devil. I guess he was thinking money,
"How much money is this gonna make?" So he was
thinking deeper things. Yet we knew we had funny
stuff, in this sequence here, or that one, and we thought,
"This'll get the old man, we're bound to get a smile
out of him." Nothing. So then you became more determined, you'd say, "We'll show the old fool—wait till
the preview." And sure enough, it would go most of
the time.

ADAMSON: But that wouldn't change his mind?

AVERY: No, he would say, "Well, it went off pretty good," and
that's it. Really, you know, it was a game of poker. If
the producer starts going up and praising his director,
boy! In a few weeks, you'll say, "What the hell, I know
I'm worth more. . . ." So it's a game of poker with them.

For a while, you know, we had to fight like a fool
to even get our names on them! Your producer doesn't
want anyone to know that you're responsible. He wants
them to think he's responsible.

ADAMSON: I also noticed it's "supervision." You're not credited
with having directed anything.

AVERY: No. That was Warners. Then we all rebelled. "Supervision" sounds like you're a personnel man. But we finally
got "direction" credit, and then they were afraid that
we would join the Directors Guild. Well, of course,
we wanted to get in, but the Guild wouldn't have us.
They wouldn't let a cartoon director be a member.

In the write-ups, they would write up the cartoon
and mention Quimby and maybe, sometime, the story
guy, but never the director. We had a clipping service,
and these people would grade cartoons—"Good, Funny,
Very good, Excellent"—and eventually, on their own,
they started listing the directors. And then if they liked
one in particular they'd put (in) a little paragraph
about it, and what a good job the director did here.
Which we were tickled to death with, gee whiz, we'd
run in and show it to the old man and he'd say, "Yeah,
yeah." You know, he didn't want to see a good write-

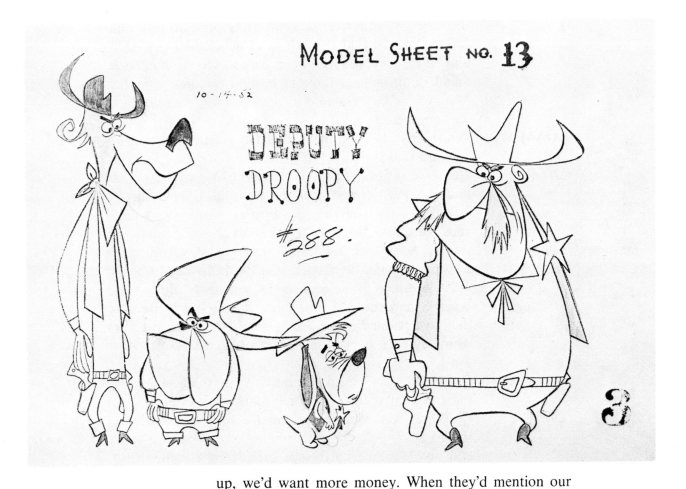

up, we'd want more money. When they'd mention our names, oh, it floored him! Didn't mention his, oh, Gee!

ADAMSON: Why did you turn from Fred Avery into Tex Avery?

AVERY: Well, at Warners they wanted more dignity, or something, so it had to be Fred, your real name. And then the next move I made, to Metro, they let me take the name of Tex, which everyone knew me by. When I came out here they tagged me Tex because I had the twang. So then, after I was acquainted with the business, everyone knew me by that name, they didn't know "Fred," so I said what the hell, I'll keep it. But when you get around sixty and they call you Tex, it's pretty childlike. So now I'm going back to Fred.

ADAMSON: Tell me something about Heck Allen, your story man at MGM.

AVERY: Oh, he was a great guy. He was with Harman and Ising before me, and I retained him. Wasn't too much on gags, but on the story line he helped me a heck of a lot.

ADAMSON: Wasn't too much on gags? Considering your movies are ninety-five percent gags, he wouldn't seem to be of much use.

AVERY: Well, you need something to hang them on. Heck Allen was a good man to have around. He was the best gag man I ever worked with. He later became a terrific writer—started writing for pulp magazines, and from there he got an article in *True*. He's quite an historian, Indian lore and all that bit, and he studied that stuff, and he read, read, read. Then he got into the hardback, and I think he sold three to motion pictures. *The Tall Men,* with Clark Gable, was one, and *MacKenna's Gold* was another.

ADAMSON: (Outraged) Do you mean that Heck Allen wrote *MacKenna's Gold?*

AVERY: He wrote it as a novel and they bought it from him. He has two pen names, Will Henry and Clay Fisher. I talked to him over the phone after *MacKenna's Gold* came out, and he said, "Look, Tex, tell me what you think." So I saw him later, and I said, "Too much chase, too many hoofbeats, and the Indian girl tried to kill the white girl about three too many times." He laughed and said, "Yeah, those damn fools!" Because they just padded it. I said, "I didn't think those horses would ever get out of the canyon." He said, "No, neither did I."

ADAMSON: Did Heck Allen's background have anything to do with the fact that you did so many cartoon Westerns?

AVERY: Oh, sure. And Westerns seemed easy. I like Westerns; so did Heck Allen. People always like Westerns—they still do. There was a theater called The Hitching Post, right across from the Pantages, that ran nothing but Westerns. There was a line out there every night, you couldn't get in there.

ADAMSON: How did you work up your stories?

AVERY: One would come from a joke or something. Or some situation that we would milk. Like the bad luck deal. Goodness, you can go on and on and on and on! It takes two guys to kick ideas around. "What do you think of this?" and "Where can we put Droopy?" Perhaps we've just seen a Western and we'll say, "Let's try one," and things would evolve. And there were many times we'd get stuck and couldn't continue, and we'd put the gags aside and try it again later. I never had any set way of building a story. They would come so many different ways. Sometimes we'd go back over our notes and find an idea that had a good beginning and no ending, and we'd finally solve it. The story man was there continually. While I was busy with the animators he'd be typing out little synopses, and we might pick one out and kick it around. We'd go all around the bush, oh, good night! Then we'd let it rest for a few days, try something else, and come back to it.

172

Most of our pressure was hitting the deadlines. The studio didn't need the films that soon, they always had a backlog, but it was just the idea that you were contracted to make so many a year. If we found ourselves coming back to something for a couple of weeks, and we still couldn't solve it, then we'd revert to a series of spot gags, like DETOURING AMERICA or THE HOUSE OF TOMORROW. You could always find spot gags. Looking back, the weaker cartoons are the ones that you just couldn't solve completely, but you had to go ahead with them.

ADAMSON: How do you mean, "solve"?

AVERY: The real problem was to build up to a laugh finish. Gosh! If you build up to a point and then the last gag is nothing, you've hurt your whole show, audience-wise. So in all of them we attempted to be sure that we had a topper.

ADAMSON: I saw CAR OF TOMORROW last weekend.

AVERY: Oh . . . not too good. That was one of those deals when you get stuck, and just do spot gags.

ADAMSON: Well, are the storyboards for those done in a big hurry, like a couple of days?

AVERY: Yeah, yeah.

ADAMSON: There wasn't anything *wrong* with CAR OF TOMOR-ROW.

AVERY: No, but see, there was nothing to build to. Boom—you've got your last gag, which maybe you think is the strongest. Like a deck of cards, you pick the highest one, put it down at the end. It might be a little entertaining, but there's nowhere to go. Those were definitely cheaters, and I hated to make 'em, but we'd get stuck once in a while.

See, you had a footage quota to meet, there, and the Front End would really cry if you didn't make a deadline. You sit there and you throw out one story and you'll throw out another, and you get so far with another, and you can't go further—junk that—until you get down to, say, maybe in another week or ten days, your animators need work, and you've gotta have work for them or the whole company falls apart. Once in a while, we would get right down to the line, and I wasn't ready with my story, so my animators who had finished the previous picture (two of 'em anyway—the other three are still working) would come in Monday morning and say, "We need work," and I'd say, "We aren't ready for you, we haven't finished our story." So, Hanna and Barbera would say, "Well, we'll carry him for a week for you," which would take a little pressure

"Fred" Avery, shortly after his move to MGM.

174

Avery and Quimby at the drawing board: LONESOME LENNY on deck.

off. And then vice versa—we'd take their man when they got caught.

ADAMSON: I noticed that your stronger films seem to have one central idea behind them, and then simply variations on a single gag.

AVERY: It's usually a simple formula, and it doesn't have to get complicated. The Roadrunner's the same darn thing—the situation, and then just different ways of trying to catch the Roadrunner. The beauty of that thing was all the intricate building and the big deal to catch this guy—and all he did was run through, and Pow! Ideal! And like our little BAD LUCK BLACKIE: The cat actually never did anything. He just ran through. That was his job.

ADAMSON: BAD LUCK BLACKIE is an amazing story. It has three threads to it, and they seem to be very carefully worked out together.

AVERY: They weren't, Joe, they weren't too carefully work out. Those things just started falling! That particular picture we built in no time, I'd say three or four days. Instead of two or three weeks. But it jelled very fast; in fact, we threw stuff out. We had more than we needed. And the one down at Lantz's came very easy, THE LEGEND OF ROCKABYE POINT—that came fast. They weren't labored over. I'll tell you, CRAZY MIXED-UP PUP was labored over a bit. A lot of it was timing. Because if you take too much time, why, you've lost it. But some were very rough, and others, as I say, they just came fast.

ADAMSON: Was it the good ones that came fast?

AVERY: Most of the time.

ADAMSON: Like LITTLE RURAL RIDING HOOD?

AVERY: No, that was labored over. All the Red Riding Hoods were labored. Boy, it took time.

ADAMSON: Why was that?

AVERY: I don't know. We were dealing with a human, for one thing. According to the censors there on the lot, we had to watch bestiality, an animal against a human female—so they couldn't get close. Those were tough to keep clean!

If I had a record, you could go back to the weakest pictures we made there, you'd find that perhaps five weeks were spent on story. And six weeks is the limit. You'll find one where the story's completed in two weeks, most of the time you'll find that's a good cartoon. Because it comes easy, it moves right out. But usually what caused a weak cartoon was a matter of schedule—you got so far and you had to continue, good or bad.

176

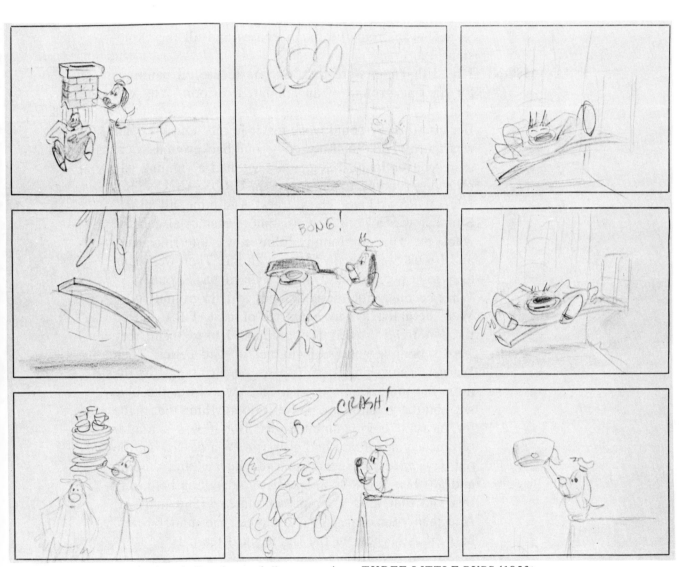

Avery's "crude roughs": a scene from THREE LITTLE PUPS (1953).

ADAMSON: If you do something like SH-H-H-H-H, or SYMPHONY IN SLANG, or Jones with his ONE FROGGY EVENING—complete departures from the Bugs Bunnys and the Daffy Ducks and the Droopys, what kids go to cartoons to see—were you trying to get away from those things, or was it just to get a break from them?

AVERY: Just a break. No, we weren't attempting to get away from them, but we would always try to get something fresh. We'd get a kick out of some of these . . . SYMPHONY IN SLANG . . . we were practically the only ones that laughed at 'em. But it was fun, you know, to get away from the damn chases and all the explosions. . . .

ADAMSON: I read that you were the first one to use oil paintings for the background of an animated cartoon. Why was that?

AVERY: Because the guy could work faster in oils, and his color was more vivid. In those days, our backgrounds were more conventional. I remember we had a running gag on a dog running to the forest, in CROSS-COUNTRY DETOURS—"Trees, trees, trees! And mine, all mine!" But that was all oils, the Rushmore memorial and the whole bit. This guy Johnny Johnson was a terrific artist, and I took him over to Metro with me. Then we swung over to watercolor and more stylized backgrounds.

ADAMSON: What accounts for these changes in background style?

AVERY: Well, actually, it was a matter of cost. UPA started the new trend in their backgrounds. I liked them; they were so simple and your characters read better. Then Warners came into it, and we came into it last of the three big majors. We tried to get away from the blue sky and the green grass, and just do anything that made for pleasant color combinations. But it was a matter of time saving. If you had a prairie, or a desert—in the old days we'd put sagebrush and plateaus and shading and all this. Now, Poom! A flat color along here, and this and that, and a couple of plateaus and that's it! And then your character had to read, no matter where he was! Anywhere in the frame, he'd read.

In so many things you see today, a gag is ruined due to the busyness of the background. You want to see a firecracker, or the guy's teeth coming out or his nose falling off, and if it's cluttered up with a lot of foliage or something behind it you'll lose the gag. I see it every day in these quickies. They make the cartoons for television so fast that they don't have time to plan them. Any time that we wanted to punch something, we would never clutter it up, we would attempt to silhouette it, and

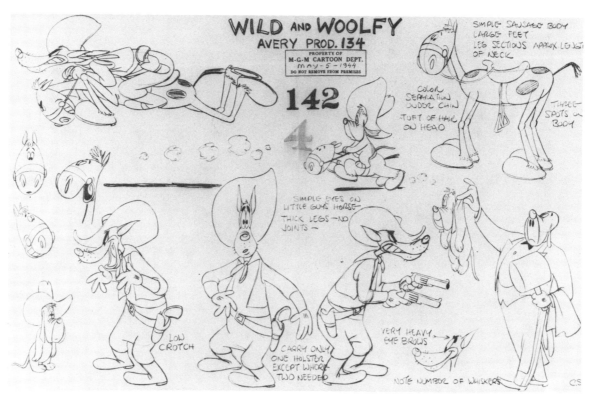

An Avery model sheet contains much of the vigor and force of expression that distinguish the finished film.

you can't miss it. I discovered that from looking at old cartoons. So many gags are also lost—and you still see it done today—from your eye following the wrong thing. Say you've got a fellow dancing on the right side of the screen, and you've got your gag working over on the left side: if this fellow on the right is too active, then your eye remains on him; you'll lose track of what's going on over here. We learned that early—if you've got two people working in a scene, slow one of them down until he's static if you want to build up to a laugh with the other one.

We used to go to softness to make 'em read; a lot of airbrush work, always fuzz, to soften any hard lines in the background. And that was the way of sharpening up the character, because he had a black line around him. And Disney used to do it, his men were masters at making anything read. You have to be conscious of that.

ADAMSON: As a director, how many sketches would you normally make for an action?

AVERY: Well, you've got six hundred feet of film, and you'd give them at least a drawing every foot, so there's about six hundred drawings. Perhaps more if there are two characters working. These are rough sketches—the positions and the expressions. At times you'd have a model man, and he would take your crude roughs and sharpen them

179

Some of the complicated paperwork that animation necessitates: these are back-grounds from THE FIRST BAD MAN (1955).

up. Then from there they would go to an animator, and if he was clever enough he could improve those again. So you've got the third refinement. The animator was working from drawings made by the model man, based on my originals. I don't think the model man ever got any credit, though he may have been listed as an animator. Then, later on, they abandoned model men and went right from the directors to the animators. For a while, at Metro, there was one model man who did all the models on model sheets—one character with every expression and in every position. Then, I would take my roughs and give them to the animators, and they would work from the model sheets. Which worked out fine.

ADAMSON: Why did you take a year off from 1952 to 1953?

AVERY: Oh, I got too wrapped up in my work. I tried to do everything myself. Normally a director will rough the scenes out and time them, and then check over the completed scenes and make changes for the boys. But I attempted to put so much on paper, the way I saw it and the way I wanted it, pinning it right down to the frame, that it required a lot of work—Saturdays, Sundays—to keep up to schedule. I was doing all the technical stuff: pans, and getting a character in a certain spot at a certain time. I enjoyed it, but it got too rough for me. I was figuring out every little move for them, which was silly. When I came back I had a different attitude; I finally turned it over to the checkers and let them work a little. I would loosen up the scenes and let the animator take some responsibility. I didn't worry too much about the stories, and they came out just as well. And, as a result, it meant a few more changes after I saw the stuff, but it was much easier. After the rest we had a beautiful start, and then they decided to close the place.

ADAMSON: You also seem to have cut back production during the war years.

AVERY: That was an attempt to save the talent. Metro had a lot of power and they would get us these training films. We would do so much for the army and navy and still make a skeleton number of theatrical cartoons, thereby a lot of the fellows got deferments.

ADAMSON: What kind of things did you do?

AVERY: We had Bertie the Bomber. An animated plane and a tank, and we put a little personality into it. But then always coming back to the matter of how to load this bomber and tread waves and maneuver and so forth.

ADAMSON: Is this a character, Bertie the Bomber? Was it a plane?

AVERY: Yeah, it was a plane.

ADAMSON: With teeth and eyes?

AVERY: It had eyelashes and red lips. But you got to put a little something in there, or the boys'll go to sleep. So we attempted a little humor, as much as we could get and still stay in the same vein.

ADAMSON: How was this worked out with the army?

AVERY: They had a script. They'd send a man out, and of course we'd draw up a storyboard. They would have sequences there where they'd want the bomber to go up to thirty thousand feet and wheeze a little, and they're saying,

181

"Well, at thirty thousand feet, you got to watch the de-icing," and we attempted to get little gags on de-icing. And if you do this incorrectly, why, your load will shift to the rear. And it was a challenge; a serious subject, trying to put a little humor in it.

ADAMSON: Where did the gags come from, basically?

AVERY: Our gag men. We would get with the sergeant. Of course he was a good audience. After working on all this technical stuff, he would be. He'd say, "Well, now, how can you show the load shifting to the rear of the plane?" And we'd sketch out Bertie, her little fanny dragging. And, oh man, it kills him! He says, "That'll keep them awake!"

Actually, we were thinking of the army when we made the first one in that RED HOT RIDING HOOD group. We had the sergeant there to help plan the training films, and when we finished cutting and dubbing the first RED HOT RIDING HOOD, we got it down to the projection room where we always ran the picture for the producer and the whole group. And the sergeant spotted the thing and he roared. We had it rather rough on the reaction of the wolf, you know, steam coming out from under his collar and all that. When the censor saw it, he said, "Boy, he's getting too worked up," so we had to trim and juggle and cut back. It got back to Washington, to some colonel or whatnot, that the censor had cut out quite a bit on us. Finally, Louis B. Mayer got a telegram from the colonel, saying that he wanted an uncut version of a RED HOT RIDING HOOD cartoon for his personnel overseas. The studio dug around, and I don't know how many prints they gave him but, man, it went over great overseas!

ADAMSON: Did the Hays Office really get concerned about a wolf and a girl getting too close?

AVERY: Oh my, yeah!

ADAMSON: But Droopy runs off with the girl at the end of WILD AND WOOLFY!

AVERY: Yeah, but there seemed to be a little difference. A "Hollywood wolf," in those days, was considered a real man-about-town: "He's a wolf." He chases girls. So that had a lot to do with it. A little fat chubby dog was different. But showing body heat, the steam coming out of the collar, and the tongue rolling out—it's suggestive stuff, in a way, you know? Sometimes we would just stiffen him out in mid-air; he'd make a take and his whole body would stiffen out like an arrow! And they cut that one out on us. On the first one, they cut out quite a bit.

ADAMSON: They didn't cut the others?

AVERY: No, then we learned. They'd told us what we couldn't do. From there on we would have to write a synopsis of every

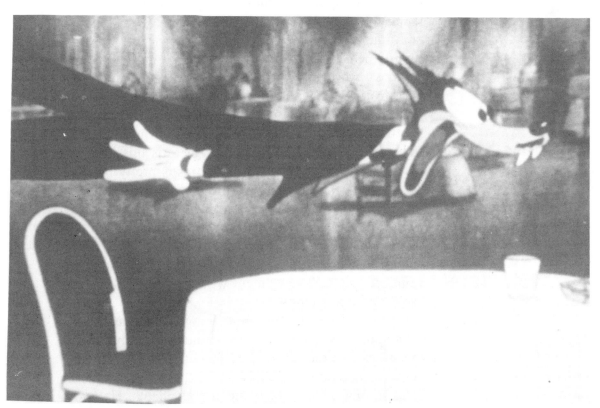

RED HOT RIDING HOOD: Avery claims this erection caricature was cut, but it still survives in most 16mm prints.

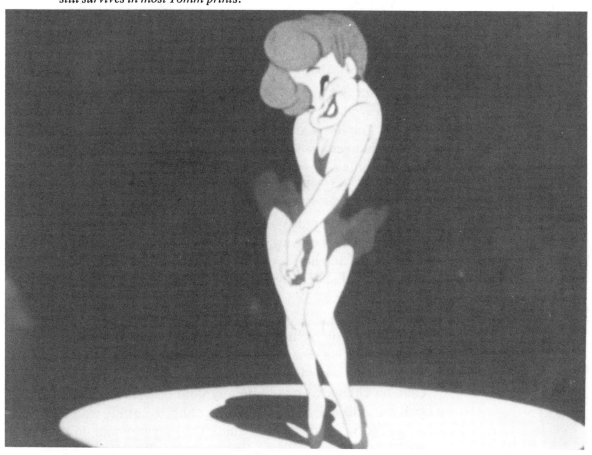

Some of Preston Blair's animation of the dancing girl in RED HOT RIDING HOOD (1943).

scene, and the action. Poom! It'd go to the Hays Office. It was the old deal. If we had one suggestive gag there, or one that was partially suggestive but we felt was very funny, then in there we would inject perhaps three that we knew we couldn't get by with. And then it'd come back from Hays, well, they'd check out in the red pencil, "This goes," then they come down here, we threw in another one down here, "This goes," get on down here, "This has to go!" And hidden in there is this little one that we liked. They'd say, "Well, this is pretty bad, but we'll let this one slip by." We did that time after time on those Riding Hood deals. I don't know where we learned it. But they do start whacking your script, and then they start feeling a little sorry for you, perhaps. "They aren't gonna have any picture left here! We'll leave this one in."

ADAMSON: I noticed the girl's movement was very lifelike. Did you use Rotoscope on those?

AVERY: No. Preston Blair did the whole thing; he was very clever on anatomy and dances. He wouldn't let anyone else touch her! He did all the girl sequences. He'd gained a lot of experience on FANTASIA, he did a lot of the dancing of the crocodiles and the elephants. He had a touch for dancing. And he couldn't dance worth his tail —big, lumbering guy! But, boy, he could really make 'em dainty.

ADAMSON: Why didn't you use Rotoscope?

AVERY: Oh, I don't know, it was costly, and required a lot more time. You'd have to shoot the film and then go back and animate it. But at Schlesinger's, we got a stripper for one of the travelogue things; we went downtown and brought her up. The line was, "Of course you people know that a lizard changes its skin once a year." Here's this little lizard running along, and then she suddenly gets up and "Da da da DA!" But there, we had the real babe! And she was undressing. She'd take off her sleeve here (the skin) and toss it out. We Rotoscoped her action to fit the lizard. Shaped the lizard like a girl, took off her skin and she was just a lighter green. It got a great laugh, too.

ADAMSON: I wonder if that's really a sensual act among lizards.

AVERY: No, snakes do it. What the heck, we couldn't animate a snake.

ADAMSON: (Shocked) You mean the lizard doesn't do it?

AVERY: I don't think so. But we knew a snake did, and I think the gag came up, "Let's have a snake striptease." But we couldn't change a snake into any kind of a shape, like a girl, but a lizard, with the two legs and the arms, would get by, so we switched it. I think the narrator said, "Of course you all know that a lizard changes its skin once a year." We had to plant it.

The Rotoscoped Lizard: CROSS-COUNTRY DETOURS (1940).

ADAMSON: Did you ever re-cut a film after a sneak preview if you found you weren't getting the laughs you wanted?

AVERY: No, we hardly ever changed anything. Once in a very great while. I think it was a matter of cost. Once the producers put their money into it, they didn't want to change the negative or anything. But we would get quite an opinion just by running the pencil reel. We would always shoot a reel of pencil tests, and then we'd call the entire group in—inkers, painters, office workers, secretaries—and it was like a sneak preview. You could tell whether it was any good or not. By golly, you might have a hundred people there, and perhaps six animators and the gag man and myself; maybe ten of us out of a hundred knew the show. There, we could change it. We could say, 'Well, we're too slow here on this gag," or, "This one just doesn't work, let's pull it." Thereby, before it was inked and painted and put on film, we were quite sure whether we had a good picture.

ADAMSON: Were you thinking of children when you made most of your cartoons, or were you thinking of an adult audience?

These animation drawings from SCREWBALL SQUIRREL illustrate the fate of cuddly creatures in Avery's universe.

AVERY: Oh, we didn't think. I guess I leaned more toward an adult audience, even with the early Bugs Bunnys. I tried to do something I thought I would laugh at if I were to see it on the screen, rather than worry about "Will a ten-year-old laugh at this?" Because we couldn't top Disney, and we knew he had the kid following, so we went for adults and young people. That's why I got away from the fuzzy bunny things. You know, with cutie cuddly squirrels and little mice singing and all that bit. They started getting rougher later on, but at first everyone leaned

toward the cute things. With little attempts at gags, but nothing slapstick to the point of hitting a guy in the head and having his teeth fall out.

Chuck Jones started out doing real cute things. He tried to compete with Disney. He finally saw the light, you know, and then he started gagging. But he had a cute little mouse, Sniffles, and he did the little fuzzy wuzzy things for a while there, then he got off it.

Then at MGM we built up to a different type of humor, a faster humor. You can see them evolve. Put all my cartoons together and start running 'em, and, well, it looks like speeding up film. You run the *old* stuff (I still call my stuff "new"), and they would take thirty feet of film to do a gag. We found that we could cut it down and do it in eight feet and it would still read. And it's funnier. You take television today, you can get a gag in six frames of film—bing-bing-bing-bing-BANG! We gunned things up to the point where we could get twice as much stuff in a cartoon, getting from one situation right into another. A guy would no sooner get hit with an anvil than he takes one step over and falls in a well. Keep them going, and it builds up for your audience. My golly!

ADAMSON: It seems to me that a lot of the things you did wouldn't be funny if they weren't happening so fast.

AVERY: That's right. I think I started that faster trend. We started filling in more gags. Prior to that, they felt you had to have a story. Finally we got to where the "story" was just a string of gags with a "topper." I found out the eye can register an action in five frames of film. Five frames of film at twenty-four a second, so it's roughly a fifth of a second to register something, from the screen to your eye to the brain. I found out, if I wanted something just to barely be seen, five frames was all it needed. What would ruin it would be two or three seconds of film . . . no, you'd have nothing. Say we had an anvil falling, we would bring it in perhaps four or five frames before the hit, that's all you need—Djuuuuuu . . . Bam! it's there, and you don't know where in the hell it came from. It makes that gag that much funnier. If you saw this thing coming down, and you panned down with it, and it hits—uh uh. But I kept speeding up my timing and I think I was followed, with the Roadrunner and that stuff.

My prime reason was—on the good ones—we wanted to get more gags in. I said, "We'll time this as fast as we can because we've got so much more to come! And if it doesn't go in the test reel, I'll pad it; I'll add drawings to it, and we'll take out some other gags." But we found that these things would all read.

Avery going over a bar sheet with Scott Bradley, music director for the MGM cartoons.

If you can read a line drawing of an anvil falling, in a pencil test, you know that you can read it in the film because it becomes a solid. We ran tests years ago on a bouncing ball in a line drawing, and it looks fast. Get a girl to paint it in . . . the damn thing floats! Because you've got a solid, rather than a line movement. If you have a little line, that tends to go fast; but you fill it in, it slows it up at least a third. Another thing we learned.

ADAMSON: What would you say your impossible style of comedy derived from?

AVERY: A lot of it comes back from those old slapstick comedies. Chaplin—I guess everybody's copied him. You can see

Rehearsal: Spike as he appeared in animators' sketches, with his co-star, an unnamed cat.

some of the things they contrived with wires and so forth to get impossible gags—Mack Sennett with his Ford going between two trolleys. We found out early that if you did something with a character, either animal or human or whatnot, that couldn't possibly be rigged up in live action, why then you've got a guaranteed laugh. If a human can do it, a lot of times it isn't funny in animation. Or even if it is funny, a human could do it funnier. They attempted to make a Laurel and Hardy cartoon series. Well, goodness, you can't copy their reactions and all of that. But if you can take a fellow and have him get hit on the head and then he cracks up like a piece of china, then you know you've got a laugh! Because they cannot do it live!

I would also say that magazine cartoons were a big influence. Virgil Partch started going crazy like that—

190

having a guy taking a shower inside a helmet, just his head sticking out. There have been times when a magazine cartoon has built into a funny cartoon gag—twisting it, and switching it around, changing the situation or something. Or distortion, we've gotten a lot out of distortion, a character getting into something he couldn't possibly get into—a milk bottle or something. You couldn't possibly do that with Charlie Chaplin, get him in a milk bottle.

ADAMSON: Is this something you worked at deliberately—"Let's do a lot of things that couldn't possibly happen"?

AVERY: I guess we did. "Let's go wilder than we did last time." Faster, too.

ADAMSON: In doing the sort of gags that other cartoon directors very carefully refrained from doing, didn't you find yourself in trouble?

Spike in the finished animation drawings.

191

AVERY: Well, you've got to build. . . .

ADAMSON: Friz Freleng insists that you always have to believe in the character as a living being, and as soon as he falls apart and puts himself back together you don't believe in him anymore.

AVERY: No, I don't think he's right. Because I've done it so much, my goodness. But I don't know. It never seemed to bother us, as far as demolishing a character or making him appear unbelievable. It never seemed to bother anybody else, either.

     You know how a little hair will get in the projector gate when you're watching home movies and twitter and jump and jerk? That used to happen in the early movie houses, too. Well, we threw one in a cartoon, and for a hundred feet, spasmodically, regardless of our continuity, this little hair would jump around the bottom of the screen and twirl and twitch and disappear. We would bring it back, and bring it back, and finally in the middle of the scene one of the characters stopped and reached down and grabbed the hair and went ping! and threw it out of the scene, and they went on with the action. Well, that got a roar.*

     The night of the preview, the manager of the theater came back and said, "Hey, our projectionist just told me he had a heck of a time with that hair. He says he was trying to get it off all through the running of the picture." Then Metro started getting letter after letter from various theaters, saying, "For God's sake, do something about this hair, it's been running our projectionist crazy!" The studio had to put a red sticker on every print of that film, and it said, "Projectionists Notice: The hair that you will see on the screen is on the film, don't try blowing it out of the projector gate."

ADAMSON: Were you ever criticized for the quantities of violence you put in your films?

AVERY: No. Not in those days. I see it come up today due to the gun laws and all that—violence, violence, violence. Why, it was violence with us all the way through! Of

---

* The film in question is THE MAGICAL MAESTRO, and it's a brilliant example of getting a gag to read properly. The character on the screen is, as a matter of fact, dancing rather vigorously, but as no variation is provided in the kind of dancing he's been performing for the last two minutes, your eye jumps straight to the hair the instant it appears. The animation of the hair, too, is convincing as all get-out (Avery claims it was Rotoscoped), so that when the character pulls it out, it comes as a total shock.—JA3.

course, we thought it was funny. I mean, a fellow could get hit in the head and stand there and have his whole body crack and fall in a pile and his own hands would get up and scoop it all up and put himself back together again. We found that you can get a terrific laugh out of someone just getting demolished—as long as you clean him up and bring him back to life again. It's exaggeration to the point where we hope it's funny. Because we hope the audience will say, "Well, it could never happen to a guy like that. All this shit could never fall on a guy." Those things never bothered me. We got great reaction from them, so we kept doing them. But then I've read or heard, "The Violent Era . . . This guy Avery . . . Gee whiz! He killed people!" And it never came to me that way, you know? Because they were still living; that's how I always felt. I was thinking of funny cartoons, and all of a sudden this guy calls me a *killer*. Then I look back and I think, "Yeah, I did take that fella's head off."

ADAMSON: How many people were saying things like that?

AVERY: Nobody in those days. Guys in the business never mentioned it. They'd say it was a funny cartoon and, "Gee, when he got hit on the head and broke apart—funny gag!" Nothing about "You're so violent," nothing like that.

Then there was WHAT'S BUZZIN' BUZZARD. Two hungry buzzards trying to devour each other. That was almost a gruesome thing! It was building up to something that could be terrible! Awful! He's going to bite off the guy's arm! But he never quite makes it.

(A girl enters the room, sees the two of us, and exits the room.)

AVERY: Honey, you want me?

GIRL: No—Jack Young. Excuse me.

AVERY: Do you *ever* want me?

(Flustered, the girl scampers down the hallway.)

ADAMSON: How was Droopy created?

AVERY: We built it on a voice. FIBBER McGEE AND MOLLY, the old radio show, had a funny little mush-mouth fellow, so we said, "Hell, let's put a dog to it." It was the voice we thought so much of. It was a steal; there ain't no doubt about it.

ADAMSON: Was it the same kind of character?

AVERY: No, on radio he was a human. He was a little meek guy, and it was Bill Thompson who did the voice. He couldn't give us exactly the voice he did for the show, for legal reasons, but he came close.

Just before they closed down the MGM Cartoon Department, right at the finish, we had this South Carolina wolf, with Daws Butler doing the voice. Daws Butler had quite a flock of voices. We liked that one. This wolf would never get excited—whistling the little tune—but he'd get the hell beat out of him. We'd use him in very violent action; then we'd freeze him and he'd make his crack: "Pretty smart li'l ol' dogs in there." We were very enthused about the guy—again it was the voice more than the character. He played opposite Droopy in THREE LITTLE PUPS. We previewed that thing, and even Quimby was enthused. He said, "Yes sir, them things are funny. Every time he opens his mouth, he gets a laugh."

We found that, rather than have this guy react in a terrific way, if he'd be very calm over some very dangerous situation, and just come out with some silly little line, it would break 'em up! Oh my! And he was whistling—to show how calm he was—"Jubilo," that's an old Civil War deal. There was a guy in the orchestra with little brushes on a little drum there, and we'd have the wolf whistle, and this little guy just tapped those things.

We spread it around; we said, "Boy, we've got something here!" At that time Pete Smith [maker of humorous short films for MGM] was Quimby's big buddy, and he was on the lot, and Pete had a sense of humor. Pete says, "Boy! You save that voice. I don't care what character you put with it, but you got a funny voice there." Then, BOOM, the stuff hit the fan. Metro's cartoon department folded, and Hanna and Barbera were very smart in picking that voice up. That started their HUCKLEBERRY HOUND series, man.*

After that, I went to Walter Lantz. He wanted a penguin, and I put it with a dog and we drew up some models. I think Paul Smith kicked it around; we all made suggestions on it. And we got it cute; that's what he wanted. But the penguin wasn't funny, there was nothing to it, no personality, no nothing. So I attempted to get humor—since he wanted a penguin so bad—

* Huckleberry Hound, popularized by Hanna and Barbera after they left MGM, is identical in voice and characterization to the dogcatcher in THREE LITTLE PUPS, the farmer in BILLY BOY, and the watchdog in I'M COLD. —JA3.

Chilly Willy gets transferred from drawing to cel, and loses a fair amount of soul in the process.

SH-H-H-H model sheet.

© WALTER LANTZ PRODUCTIONS, INC.

from the dumb dog, or the dumb seagull, or the dumb polar bear. Shucks, you couldn't do anything with a little fuzzy wuzzy penguin! But the cartoons weren't bad, I worked hard on them. THE LEGEND OF ROCKABYE POINT was up for the Academy Award.

ADAMSON: You also made that one called SH-H-H-H.

AVERY: Didn't go. We took that old laugh record, which was before your time, and we got rights to it. We found one in pretty good shape, and I talked Lantz into doing it. We called in a painter and inker or something, and said, "Hey, listen to this," and sat there, didn't say any-anything, and watched them. Sooner or later they start . . . a smile, then a giggle, and then they're laughing right along with it. So we said, "If we can get the audience to do that, this is great!" But it didn't do so well in the preview, because the audience felt that we were attempting to force them into laughing. Like your laugh tracks on TV—they wouldn't accept it. Aw, we were sad.

ADAMSON: Did you have to argue with Lantz to get something like that made?

196

AVERY: No, he went right along with it; it caught him, too. But then later he said, "Oh man, we sure missed it." The laugh alone, if I played it for you here, you would snicker and then really bust out. Our mistake was attempting to put gags on top of it; thereby one was competing with the other. But an experiment I always wanted to try with that thing—which would run about three minutes, the duration of the record: take it to a theater, and just pull your curtains, and no picture! Just run this track. I think your audience would start laughing, I really do. Of course, we never tried it. But attempting to analyze the picture afterwards, we thought of that—just run three minutes of that laugh and let it keep building up, and check the audience. They'd either boo and stomp to get a picture up there, or they'd join in the laughter. But it was quite an experience.

ADAMSON: I think SH-H-H-H-H is a nice cartoon.

AVERY: Well, it sure was a gamble . . . that didn't pay off.

ADAMSON: Um. . . .

AVERY: Think hard, Joe.

ADAMSON: How was Lantz to work for, in comparison with the others?

AVERY: He was all right; he had a sense of humor. He'd leave us alone until the storyboard was completed, and then he'd probably put a little something of his in there, or change a little something. It wasn't bad. He didn't want me to leave. Because immediately they got much better write-ups, and there was a different pace than what he'd been doing, you know. He'd do the same routine, one thing right after another, a carbon copy. But we went a little offbeat with him, and he appreciated it.

At that time, the Universal cartoons ran only in small houses. He told me that most of their market is abroad, that's where they make their money. They're rated much lower than the others, and they're cheaper. The big houses won't take 'em.

ADAMSON: The Lantz cartoons? Why is that?

AVERY: When Woody Woodpecker came out, they ran them in big houses, Universal houses. But then Universal at that time had quite a few theaters. Lantz talked me into a percentage deal—a salary plus a percentage of the take. And it sounded good to me. It's like an annuity, you know, it took a year or two to get anything out of them. But I tried it. I guess I made about four cartoons for him, then I started thinking about the contract. I took it to an attorney, and he said, "Oh, brother! You'll never get a dime out of this. You're getting charged for everything but the paving out in front of the studio." I was getting my percentage off the bottom instead of off the top. By the time all the charges went in, why, my goodness, there was nothing left. But I don't know, I'm not sharp at those things. So I gave up there, and went into commercials.

ADAMSON: You've been doing commercials since fifty-five?

AVERY: Well, I did a secret thing for the air force, missile thing. Thirty-minute show. No good. Too many engineers involved. Throwing missiles, launching pads, the whole bit. It was interesting. Never again.

When I was left out in the cold after twenty years of directing cartoons, I said, "Why not rest a bit?" When you're making theatrical cartoons, you're using about a half million of somebody's big fat dollars every year. And you feel that you've got to give them something. If you make a weak one, you feel, my gosh, you're letting the studio down. So, with these little minute commercials, boy, you make 'em in two weeks and you're through! No problem, no sweat. You can do a minute in a day, time it, get your voices, give it to an animator. And in three weeks you'll see it on film! Without all that pressure.

ADAMSON: What specific commercials have you been doing?

AVERY: We started out on the "Wonder where the yellow went" for Pepsodent toothpaste. We've also been doing the Raid commercials, with the little bugs. We've been doing those for . . . ever. We did a series on the Frito Bandito, a little chubby Mexican fellow. We've been doing Bugs Bunny Kool-Aids for six or seven years, and when they started doing those the agency people said, "Wonder if Avery knows how to draw Bugs Bunny." I think that's when I started making it clear just who created Bugs Bunny.

This was some time ago, and then they re-opened the account recently. And we talked with them all day —how the rabbit acts, and what he does, and what he doesn't do. And we told them what was wrong with their storyboards, that the rabbit wouldn't do that. They would have him running from the people. If he ever runs from anyone, he has a trick in mind. But they had him scared to death. So we took the board apart, and we said, "You should visualize him like Groucho Marx." If you look back at the old Grouchos, he would run, real slow, with that funny lope, but then he'd stop and make some crack. He was always in command; he knew what he was doing. And I said, "Keep that in mind, a schemer and a trickster, that might help some."

ADAMSON: Considering the current state of theatrical cartoons, I imagine it didn't hurt to get out when you did.

AVERY: What, all this cheap junk, the yak-yak-yak? It woulda broken my heart! Dialogue gags are a dime a dozen, but a good sight gag is hard to come by. Chuck's attempting to fight it, trying to cling to quality stuff. But it's all that pressure! I admire Jones; I saw him come up, and Freleng, he was directing before I was—and they still bat 'em out! Freleng knocks himself out. I don't know how they do it. It's not like it used to be. We were all young, and we had a lot of fun, making these darn things. Then it became serious business later, as we got older. It cost more money, and there was more on your shoulders. I miss the creative end of it—building the story and building the gags. I do miss the theatricals, but I'd never go back to them.

6. FILMOGRAPHY

Frederick Bean Avery was born February 26, 1908, a Pisces, in Taylor, Texas. He is a direct descendant of Judge Roy Bean, but isn't exactly sure what the lineage is. All his grandmother ever told him was, "Don't ever mention you are kin to Roy Bean. He's a no good skunk!!" Avery graduated from North Dallas High School in June, 1927, and immigrated to Southern California two years later.

This listing includes only those films actually directed by Avery. Though he worked for Walter Lantz from about 1930 to 1935 as an animator, only Avery's home-town paper ever considered his contribution a major one. Titles for this period in his work include HAM AND EGGS, 1933, and ANNIE MOVED AWAY, 1934. His influence on the gag style of these cartoons is detectable as early as THE HARE MAIL in 1931. The titles of those two cartoons Avery timed for Bill Nolan are probably TOWNE HALL FOLLIES and THE QUAIL HUNT, both 1935.

The Animation Family Tree compiled by the Canadian Cinematheque is a prodigious enterprise, though it contains a number of factual errors, among them the statement that Avery worked for Paul Terry and for Charles Mintz in New York in the early thirties. Avery himself claims that, while it would have been to his credit to have actually done this, as it happens his entire career has transpired in Los Angeles.

Rating System

Though I realize the idea of rating films is a little silly, and more appropriate to movie guides for TV viewers than a true critical appraisal, and a highly subjective task complicated by the problem of comparing films seen two months ago with some not viewed for several years, I nevertheless feel that in this instance, with a large body of work familiar at present only to a small group of *cognoscenti,* it is necessary at least to pass a provisional judgmental overview, which shall read as follows:

★★★★★   A great short film is a thing of joy forever.
★★★★   Not since the thirties has such a comic mastermind been at work in the movies.
★★★   This is a better-than-average cartoon, distinguished by a fair share of great moments.
★★   Shows talent, at least. And imagination.
★   Aw. . . .

An absence of stars indicates that the film has been unavailable for viewing.

1936-1942: Warner Brothers Cartoons. These were independently produced by Leon Schlesinger, then released by Warner Brothers Pictures, Inc., and copyrighted in the name of the Vitaphone Corporation. Dates given below are copyright dates from the Library of Congress Catalogue of Copyright Entries, though they correspond roughly to actual release dates.

Though all pains have been taken to ensure accuracy in this list, it is possible that there may actually be an error or two, as it was put together from the Catalogue of Copyright Entries, the few existing records of the Warner Brothers Studios, and Tex Avery's memory. Not a one of these, unfortunately, is fully complete or fully accurate, and titles are in the process of being added and subtracted as we go to press.

Where possible, credits have been transcribed directly from the films. Many of these cartoons, however, have been re-released in Warners' "Blue Ribbon" series, and no longer boast any credits at all. It should also be remembered that Warners' cartoons under Schlesinger's aegis are notorious for bearing false or misleading credits. One animator is given credit for the work of three or four. One story man gets his name on the film, while it was usually a stable of "gag men," in the Mack Sennett sense, who contributed material. Though Avery (like all other directors under Schlesinger) was given a paltry "Supervision" credit, his function was that of an animation director and should not be considered any differently. In some instances, the director has been given no credit whatsoever, and it has taken diligent research to ascertain authorship of the film.

Although credits are skimpy and it is difficult to determine the full extent of his participation, Mel Blanc began working for the Warner Brothers' Studio in 1937, and eventually provided most of the voices heard in the cartoons.

Except where noted, all films were made in color. Some of those designated "black and white" have recently been distributed to television with color added by a recent electronic process, but I can't help that.

1936

GOLDDIGGERS OF '49 ★★ (Porky and Beans)
Supervision: Fred Avery; Animation: Charles Jones, Robert Clampett. Looney Tunes. (Black and White) January 6, 1936.

Today this looks as primitive as the strange version of "Porky Pig" it features: a giant fat hog who keeps shouting "Whoopie" and has a slit down his back like a piggy bank. About goldmining, rather than dancing on Broadway, and "Beans" wins Porky's daughter in the end.

THE BLOW-OUT ★★ (Porky Pig)
Supervision: Fred Avery; Animation: Charles Jones and Sidney Sutheraland; Musical Score: Bernard Brown. Looney Tunes. (Black and White) April 24, 1936.

Porky chases the Mad Bomber all over town returning his bombs to him, hoping to receive a tip for his pains. This cartoon, one of the two storyboards Avery worked up himself and presented to Schlesinger to land this job, is the real origin of the Ubiquity Theme developed further in TORTOISE BEATS HARE, DUMB-HOUNDED, and NORTHWEST HOUNDED POLICE.

PLANE DIPPY ★★★ (Porky Pig)
Supervision: Fred Avery; Animation: Sid Sutherland, Virgil Ross; Musical Score: Bernard Brown. Looney Tunes. (Black and White) April 30, 1936.

Porky wants to learn how to fly, and becomes the victim of a robot plane obeying instructions from a pack of heedless youth playing with their dog.

I'D LOVE TO TAKE ORDERS FROM YOU ★
Words and Music by: Warren and Dubin; Supervision: Fred Avery; Musical Score: Norman Spencer; Animation: Bob Clampett, Cecil Surry. Merrie Melodies. May 25, 1936.

The title refers to the aspirations of a baby scarecrow to be like his dad. Just how it is supposed to refer to that is unclear.

MISS GLORY ★★
(For years my research on this title was yielding contradictory information: the cartoon was either called "Miss Glory" or "Page Miss

"MISS GLORY"
A MERRIE MELODY SONG CARTOON
VITAPHONE # 3771
REL. Nº 1404

A
LEON
SCHLESINGER
CARTOON

Glory," and would be alphabetized under one title while devotees were clinging to the other. When I finally saw the film, I found the words "Miss Glory" boldly emblazoned across the top of the title card, with a tiny, apologetic "Page" crammed in on top of that. Now I'm more confused than I was before. Seeing the actual title card only destroys the certainty of either guess. Looks to me like a deliberate attempt to baffle scholars.) Producer: Leon Schlesinger; Words and Music by Warren and Dubin; Modern art conceived and designed by Leadora Congdon. Merrie Melodies. June 9, 1936.

Abner, Hickville Hotel bellhop, falls asleep waiting for Miss Glory, and dreams that Hickville is New York and its populace a New Yorker cartoon choreographed by Busby Berkeley. Avery says, "I think I was forced to make it. But forget it. It was lousy." It isn't that lousy, but it would not be uncharitable to forget it. An attempt to integrate "art deco" style into the techniques of animation results in a few interesting effects.

I LOVE TO SINGA ★★

Supervision: Fred Avery; Animation: Charles Jones, Virgil Ross; Music: Norman Spencer. Merrie Melodies. August 18, 1936.

Professor Owl's offspring hatch out of their eggs not only with musical ability inborn but with instruments. The one who performs pop music is nearly driven from the nest, and his swing breaks in on his serious lessons like Avery's crazy humor trying to burst out of a pseudo-Disney cartoon.

PORKY THE RAIN MAKER ★★ (Porky Pig)

Supervision: Fred Avery; Animation: Cecil Surry, Sid Sutherland; Music: Norman Spencer. Looney Tunes. (Black and White) December 19, 1936.

The gags work against the story in this tale of a drought on Porky's father's farm cured by Rain Pills purchased from a medicine show hawker.

THE VILLAGE SMITHY ★★ (Porky Pig)

Supervision: Fred Avery; Animation: Sid Sutherland, Cecil Surry; Musical Direction: Carl W. Stalling. Looney Tunes. (Black and White) December 19, 1936.

Porky as the blacksmith's assistant. Avery places this film as the first use of an off-screen narrator in a cartoon. "The only thing Disney ever stole from us."

MILK AND MONEY ★★★ (Porky Pig)

Supervision: Fred Avery; Animation: Charles Jones, Virgil Ross; Music: Carl W. Stalling; Produced by Leon Schlesinger. Looney Tunes. (Black and White) December 28, 1936.

A simplified version of the plot for the Marx Brothers' A DAY AT THE RACES, which came out the next year: Porky's father will lose his farm if he doesn't come into a fortune in the next twenty-four hours, and Porky's milkwagon nag comes to the rescue in a race, with Hank Horsefly assuming the role later filled by Douglas Dumbrille.

DON'T LOOK NOW ★

Supervision: Fred Avery; Animation: Robert Clampett, Joe D'Igalo; Music: Carl W. Stalling. Merrie Melodies. December 30, 1936.

Dan Cupid and A Little Devil battle it out, and it's a toss-up for the Audience Apathy Sweepstakes.

PORKY THE WRESTLER ★★★★ (Porky Pig)

Supervision: Fred Avery; Animation: Charles Jones, Elmer Wait; Music: Carl W. Stalling. Looney Tunes. (Black and White) December 30, 1936.

Porky is mistaken for the Challenger and ends up in the ring opposite the Champion.

PICADOR PORKY ★★★ (Porky Pig)
Supervision: Fred Avery; Animation: Charles Jones, Sid Sutherland;
Music: Carl W. Stalling. Looney Tunes (Black & White) May 3, 1937.

Porky enters the bullfight ring ostensibly for a fixed match with a
costume party bull, but, in a plot twist reminiscent of Chaplin's CITY
LIGHTS, his conspirators are replaced at the last minute by a hostile
specimen of the genuine article.

I ONLY HAVE EYES FOR YOU ★★
Supervision: Fred Avery; Animation: Bob Clampett, Virgil Ross; Music: Carl W. Stalling. Merrie Melodies. May 18, 1937.

Unsuccessful in fooling his lady love into thinking he can sing
like the Ventriloquist who is hiding in the ice wagon, the iceman mar-
ries the girl who can cook. A cast of birds.

PORKY'S DUCK HUNT ★★★★ (Porky Pig; Daffy Duck)
Supervision: Fred Avery; Animation: Virgil Ross, Robert Cannon;
Music Score: Carl W. Stalling. Looney Tunes. (Black and White)
July 7, 1937.

Porky goes duck hunting and meets Daffy Duck for the first time.
An historic occasion.

UNCLE TOM'S BUNGALOW ★★
Supervision: Fred Avery; Animation: Virgil Ross, Sid Sutherland; Musical Score: Carl W. Stalling. Merrie Melodies. July 12, 1937.

Lampoon of a familiar story. "My body might belong to you, but
my soul belongs to Warner Brothers," says Uncle Tom.

AIN'T WE GOT FUN ★★★
Supervision: Fred Avery; Animation: Charles Jones, Bob Clampett;
Musical Score: Carl W. Stalling. Merrie Melodies. August 2, 1937.

An old curmudgeon is cruel to his cat, but thinks better of it
when a swarm of mice overtake his house and treat him like Farmer
Alfalfa.

DAFFY DUCK AND EGGHEAD ★★★ (Daffy Duck and Egg-
head)
Supervision: Fred Avery; Story: J. B. Hardaway; Animation: Virgil
Ross; Music Score: Carl W. Stalling. Merrie Melodies. November 26,
1937. (The Duck sings "The Merry-Go-Round Broke Down," the
Looney Tunes theme song.)

Daffy is being hunted by Egghead, until finally the little ducks in
white suits come to take him away, and they go hopping and hoo-hooing
to the horizon together. Egghead gets exasperated with a member of
the audience and shoots him: the Death Scene is one for the books.

EGGHEAD RIDES AGAIN ★★ (Egghead)
Supervision: Fred Avery; Animation: Paul Smith, Irven Spence; Musical Direction: Carl W. Stalling. Merrie Melodies. November 29, 1937.

You all remember when Egghead rode before. "Today I am a

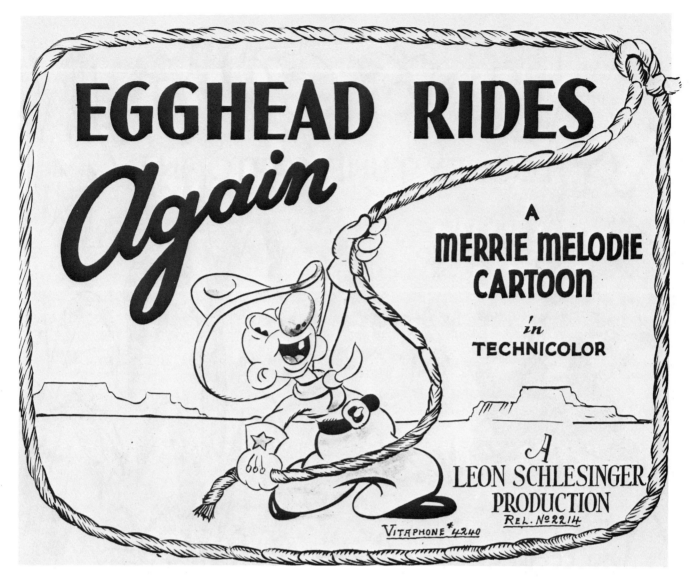

man," says Egghead, applying for a job at the Bar None Ranch. Tomorrow a turnip.

A SUNBONNET BLUE ★★
Supervision: Fred Avery; Animation: Sid Sutherland, Virgil Ross; Musical Score: Carl W. Stalling. Merrie Melodies. December 1, 1937.

Two mice in love in a hat shop. The Three Ratz Brothers sing "I Haven't Got a Hat."

PORKY'S GARDEN ★★ (Porky Pig)
Supervision: Fred Avery; Animation: Sid Sutherland, Elmer Wait; Musical Direction: Carl W. Stalling. Looney Tunes. (Black and White) 1937.

Porky grows outsized vegetables, his eyes on a garden prize, but his next-door competitor feeds his prize-hungry chickens on Porky's vegetables. Highlight is the baby chick who is picked on until he eats the spinach that transforms him into a Popeye imitation.

I WANNA BE A SAILOR ★★★
Supervision: Fred Avery. Merrie Melodies.

THE SNEEZING WEASEL ★★

Supervision: Fred Avery; Story: Cal Howard; Animation: Sid Sutherland; Music Score: Carl W. Stalling. Merrie Melodies. December 15, 1937.

A snootful of pepper rescues the baby chicks from the Evil Weasel. Later re-made by Chuck Jones in a much zingier picture called FLOP GOES THE WEASEL.

LITTLE RED WALKING HOOD ★★★ (Egghead)

Supervision: Fred Avery; Story: Cal Howard; Animation: Irven Spence; Music Score: Carl W. Stalling. Merrie Melodies. December 23, 1937.

A gagged-up rendition of the Red Riding Hood tale, with Egghead taking great pride in being the improbable hero. We know the Wolf is a malicious character because he tilts the pinball machine. The backgrounds for this were done in colored pencil, an interesting sort of departure.

1938

THE PENGUIN PARADE ★★★★
Words and Music by: Byron Gay; Supervision: Fred Avery; Story by:
J. B. Hardaway; Animation: Paul Smith; Musical Direction: Carl W.
Stalling. Merrie Melodies. August 11, 1938.

A parade of anonymous penguins whoop it up in a nightclub just
for penguins under the Northern Lights. Fats Walrus is among the
entertainers. The final number is handled fairly straight, and extremely
well.

THE ISLE OF PINGO PONGO ★★★ (Egghead)
Supervision: Fred Avery; Story: George Manuell; Animation: Irven
Spence. Merrie Melodies. September 14, 1938.

The first of Avery's "spot gag deals": the highlight of this is a
charming rendition of "Sweet Georgia Brown," performed by a quartet
of caricatured African natives. It's also the reason the film is no longer
shown on television.

A FEUD THERE WAS ★★★ (Egghead—identified as "Elmer
Fudd")
Supervision: Fred Avery; Story: Melvin Millar; Animation: Sid Sutherland. Merrie Melodies. September 24, 1938. Includes an uncredited
rendition by Roy Rogers' group "The Sons of the Pioneers."

A Texan's view of an Ozark feud. Finally settled by Egghead,
whose motorcycle calls him Elmer Fudd. A cuckoo clock awakens the
clan every morning with the sound of a cork being pulled out of a jug.
One of the characters seems to articulate Avery's credo by saying, "In
these here cartoon pictures, a fellow can do about anythaing." Good
point.

JOHNNY SMITH AND POKER-HUNTAS ★★ (Egghead)
Supervision: Fred Avery; Story: Richard Hogan; Animation: Paul
Smith; Music Director: Carl W. Stalling; Producer: Leon Schlesinger.
Merrie Melodies. October 22, 1938.

A combination of the Mayflower and Pocahontas stories, with
Capt. Johnny Smith arriving on the Mayflower, being captured by the
Indians, and rescued at the last minute by Poker-huntas.

DAFFY DUCK IN HOLLYWOOD ★★★ (Daffy Duck)
Supervision: Fred Avery; Story: Dave Monahan; Animation: Virgil
Ross; Music Director: Carl W. Stalling. Merrie Melodies. December 3,
1938.

Daffy tries to crash a Hollywood studio. He finally advances to the
Director's chair by way of the editing table, where he pulls a Vertov and
throws together his own masterwork out of stock footage with unwhole-
some-looking helpings of film cement.

CINDERELLA MEETS FELLA ★★★ (Egghead)
Supervision: Fred Avery; Story by: Ted Pierce; Animation: Virgil Ross;
Musical Direction: Carl W. Stalling. Merrie Melodies. December 8,
1938.

"Fella" turns out, by a loose definition, to mean Egghead, who thinks he's Joe Penner tonight. The fairy godmother turns the pumpkin into Santa and reindeer, then on her second try a stagecoach with horses, but hasn't got the patience to try any further and Cinderella goes to the Ball in a stagecoach. Avery's cuckoo clock gags are endless: this time nine birds emerge from the insides and holler, "It's nine o'clock!!"

HAMATEUR NIGHT ★★★★ (Egghead)

Supervision: Fred Avery; Story by: Jack Miller; Animation: Paul Smith; Musical Direction: Carl W. Stalling. Merrie Melodies. December 12, 1938. Though Egghead is not the star of this film, he figures prominently as running gag potential, as in THE ISLE OF PINGO PONGO.

It's Amateur Night at the Warmer Brothers Theater, and the laughs come from both sides of the footlights. Rejected performers are dropped through a trap door on the stage, and seem to fall past Alice's Wonderland before hitting bottom. The final shot features an audience of Eggheads, and if the prospect intimidates, try to imagine painting one of those cels.

THE MICE WILL PLAY ★★

Supervision: Fred Avery; Story: Jack Miller; Animation: Sid Sutherland; Music Director: Carl W. Stalling. Merrie Melodies. December 18, 1938. Included in The Library of Congress Film Collection, Washington, D.C. Library of Congress No. FAA6101.

"I never did any fuzzy bunnies," said Avery, till I reminded him of this one. A cute girl mouse is imprisoned as "Experiment No. 13," but is rescued by the other mice, in spite of a cat who sports a villainous moustache. In the finale, the boy and girl are "married until Judgment Day," so I suppose they're still together.

1939

A DAY AT THE ZOO ★★ (Egghead)

Supervision: Fred Avery; Story: Melvin Millar; Animation: Rollin Hamilton; Music Director: Carl W. Stalling. Merrie Melodies. March 11, 1939.

The Kalama Zoo features "the Wolf in his natural setting": at the door. Spotty spot gags.

Egghead is a takeoff on a radio comedian named Joe Penner, and the point of this parody is, today, lost on almost everybody, including me. "Some of us, including Tex, thought Egghead was a little gross."— Bob Clampett

THUGS WITH DIRTY MUGS ★★★★

Supervision: Fred Avery; Story: Jack Miller; Animation: Sid Sutherland; Music Director: Carl W. Stalling. Merrie Melodies. May 6, 1939.

The career of Killer Diller, from the First to the 112th National Bank—until he is finally arrested by Flat Foot Flanagan (with a Floy Floy), who is tipped off by a member of the audience.

BELIEVE IT OR ELSE ★★ (Egghead)

Supervision: Fred Avery; Story: Dave Monahan: Animation: Virgil

Ross; Music Director: Carl W. Stalling. Merrie Melodies. June 3, 1939.

Spot gags, many of them too slow or too labored, the funniest being a man inside a bottle building a boat *outside* the bottle.

DANGEROUS DAN McFOO ★★★
Supervision: Fred Avery; Story: Rich Hogan; Animation: Paul Smith; Music Director: Carl W. Stalling. Merrie Melodies. July 15, 1939.

Dan McFoo, though neither deaf, dumb, nor blind, turns out to be a Pinball Wizard.

DETOURING AMERICA ★★
Supervision: Fred Avery; Story by: Jack Miller; Animation: Rollin Hamilton; Musical Direction: Carl W. Stalling. Merrie Melodies. August 26, 1939. Nominated for the Academy Award, 1939.

More spot gags, mostly in the Midwest, allowing the colors to range all the way from yellow to brown. An Eskimo carries a black man off to Old Virginny.

LAND OF THE MIDNIGHT FUN ★★
Supervision: Fred Avery; Story: Melvin Millar; Animation: Charles McKimson; Music: Carl W. Stalling. Merrie Melodies. September 25, 1939.

Precious little fun in this spot gag tour of the Far North, due mostly to laborious timing on some crazy gags.

FRESH FISH ★★
Supervision: Fred Avery; Story: Jack Miller; Animation: Sid Sutherland. Merrie Melodies. November 4, 1939.

Spot gags on underwater life.

SCREWBALL FOOTBALL ★★★
Supervision: Fred Avery; Story: Melvin Millar; Animation: Virgil Ross. Merrie Melodies. December 16, 1939.

Spot gags on the gridiron.

THE EARLY WORM GETS THE BIRD ★
Supervision: Fred Avery; Story: Jack Miller; Animation: Robert Cannon; Music Direction: Carl W. Stalling; Producer: Leon Schlesinger. Merrie Melodies. December 30, 1939.

A bird who is after a worm is saved from a fox by a bee.

1940

CROSS COUNTRY DETOURS ★★★★
Supervision: Fred Avery; Story: Rich Hogan; Animation: Paul Smith; Musical Direction: Carl W. Stalling. Merrie Melodies. March 16, 1940.

The funniest of the spot-gag pictures, with beavers building the Hoover Dam, a Shirley Temple figure who frightens a gila monster off the screen, a dog who races miles to get to the Sequoias and then does a performance that will tear your heart out ("Trees! Trees! And they're mine! All mine! Ahahahahahaha!"), and a polar bear who listens unimpressed to a recounting of his fortifications against the weather and pouts, "I don't care what you say, I'm cold."

THE BEAR'S TALE ★★★

Supervision: Fred Avery; Story: J. B. Hardaway; Animation: Rod Scribner. Merrie Melodies. April 13, 1940. The Three Bears get mixed up in the story of Red Riding Hood. "Miss Goldilocks appears through the courtesy of Mervyn LeRoy Productions."

A GANDER AT MOTHER GOOSE ★

Supervision: Fred Avery; Story by: Dave Monahan; Animation: Charles McKimson; Musical Direction: Carl W. Stalling; Producer: Leon Schlesinger. Merrie Melodies. May 24, 1940.

When Avery refers to his spot-gag cartoons as "cheaters" he has pictures like this in mind. Mother Goose is credited as Technical Director.

CIRCUS TODAY ★★

Supervision: Fred Avery; Story: Jack Miller; Animation: Sid Sutherland; Music Direction: Carl W. Stalling; Producer: Leon Schlesinger. Merrie Melodies. June 22, 1940.

Spot gags go to the circus. Stay home and watch cartoons on television.

A WILD HARE ★★★★ (Bugs Bunny and Elmer Fudd)

Supervision: Fred Avery; Story: Rich Hogan; Animation: Virgil Ross; Music Direction: Carl W. Stalling. Merrie Melodies. July 27, 1940. Nominated for the Academy Award, 1940.

Elmer goes hunting Bugs. He lives to know better.

CEILING HERO ★★

Supervision: Fred Avery; Story by: Dave Monahan; Animation: Rod Scribner; Musical Direction: Carl W. Stalling; Producer: Leon Schlesinger. Merrie Melodies. August 24, 1940.

Spot gags again, with no relation whatever to Howard Hawks' CEILING ZERO—although "Calling Barranca" comes in over the pay phone in the cockpit to remind us of ONLY ANGELS HAVE WINGS.

WACKY WILD LIFE ★★

Supervision: Fred Avery; Story: Dave Monahan; Animation: Virgil Ross. Merrie Melodies. November 9, 1940.

Spot gags. Whoever wrote the title never saw the cartoon: it's about as "wacky" as DAVID COPPERFIELD.

OF FOX AND HOUNDS ★★★

Supervision: Fred Avery. Merrie Melodies. December 7, 1940.

The title card gives the following credits: Supervision: Draft No. 412; Story: Draft No. 1312; Animation: Draft No. 6102; Musical Direction: Draft No. 158 (too bad). "Which way did he go, George, which way did he go?": Avery himself plays the dumb hunting dog who asks directions from his prey.

HOLIDAY HIGHLIGHTS ★

Supervision: Fred Avery; Story by: Dave Monahan; Animation: Charles

McKimson; Musical Direction: Carl W. Stalling; Producer: Leon Schlesinger. Merrie Melodies. December 24, 1940.

Another spot-gag picture that ends with a dog making a fuss over trees.

1941

THE CRACKPOT QUAIL ★★★
Supervision: Fred Avery; Story: Rich Hogan; Animation: Robert McKimson; Music Director: Carl W. Stalling; Producer: Leon Schlesinger. Merrie Melodies. February 15, 1941.

Willoughby goes hunting a wiseguy quail who seems to want to steal some of Bugs Bunny's spotlight.

HAUNTED MOUSE ★★
Story: Michael Maltese; Animation: Sid Sutherland; Music Director: Carl W. Stalling; Producer: Leon Schlesinger. Looney Tunes. (Black and White) February 15, 1941.

A cat goes into a ghost town and is tormented by a ghost mouse. As Maltese originally wrote the ending, the cat died and became *nine* ghost cats, but in the finished film he simply becomes a ghost.

TORTOISE BEATS HARE ★★ (Bugs Bunny)
Supervision: Fred Avery; Story: Dave Monahan; Animation: Charles McKimson; Music Direction: Carl W. Stalling; Producer: Leon Schlesinger. Merrie Melodies. March 22, 1941.

Bugs is made the dupe in this misguided effort, as he races Cecil Turtle, who is bright enough to post spitting-image relatives all along the course. Bugs himself complains about it, as he stands in front of the title card, mispronouncing the credits ("Fred A-*very*"), finds out the name and the outcome of the picture, and screams, "The big bunch of joiks!"

HOLLYWOOD STEPS OUT ★★★
Supervision: Fred Avery. Merrie Melodies. 1941. Bing Crosby, Cary Grant, Johnny Weissmuller, Henry Fonda, Buster Keaton, Ned Sparks, Oliver Hardy, The Three Stooges, Peter Lorre, James Cagney, Humphrey Bogart, George Raft, Mickey Rooney, Groucho and Harpo Marx appear in caricature form. Among others. But Jimmy Stewart steals the show. Two woodcuts of scenes from this film hang in the library of the Motion Picture Academy.

PORKY'S PREVIEW ★★★ (Porky Pig)
Supervision: Fred Avery; Story: Dave Monahan; Animation: Virgil Ross; Music Director: Carl W. Stalling; Producer: Leon Schlesinger. Looney Tunes. (Black and White) April 26, 1941.

Avery's only experience with the streamlined Porky Pig. This time Porky becomes the *auteur,* with an animated cartoon he's drawn himself, consisting mostly of stick figures (as devious an animation shortcut as any I've seen). The highlight is Al Jolson singing "September in the Rain," with raindrops bouncing off his head like jelly beans.

THE HECKLING HARE ★★★ (Bugs Bunny)
Supervision: Fred Avery; Story by: Michael Maltese; Animation: Bob McKimson; Musical Director: Carl W. Stalling; Producer: Leon Schlesinger. Merrie Melodies. July 12, 1941.

For no stated purpose other than to fulfill his destiny as a hunting dog, Willoughby goes hunting Bugs. Climaxes with an extended fall: Bugs and Willoughby both screaming their throats out, tumbling through the air for miles, and finally putting on the brakes and jeering at us.

AVIATION VACATION ★
Supervision: Fred Avery; Story by: Dave Monahan; Animation: Sid Sutherland; Musical Direction: Carl W. Stalling; Producer: Leon Schlesinger. Merrie Melodies. August 9, 1941.

Hops all over the globe, making a Mt. Rushmore gag here, giving the serious treatment to an Irish ballad there. This gets my vote as the silliest of the spot-gag pictures.

ALL THIS AND RABBIT STEW ★★★ (Bugs Bunny)
Story: Dave Monahan; Animation: Virgil Ross; Music Director: Carl W. Stalling; Producer: Leon Schlesinger. Merrie Melodies. September 20, 1941. Once Avery had left the studio, it no longer seemed necessary to put his name on his unreleased films.

An unfortunate blackface caricature spoils a succession of awfully funny gags. A Rotoscope remake purportedly replaces the picaninny with Elmer Fudd.

THE BUG PARADE ★★
Producer: Leon Schlesinger; Story: Dave Monahan; Animation: Rod Scribner; Music Director: Carl W. Stalling; Merrie Melodies. October 21, 1941.

Spot gags about *insects*. There's no *limit*.

THE CAGEY CANARY ★★
Story: Michael Maltese; Animation: Robert McKimson; Music Director: Carl W. Stalling; Producer: Leon Schlesinger. Merrie Melodies. December 26, 1941. Completed by Bob Clampett, after Avery had gone.

An early model for the famous Tweetie and Sylvester battles, with a cat making earnest but unsuccessful attempts to corner a canary.

1942

ALOHA HOOEY ★★
Story by: Michael Maltese; Animation: Virgil Ross; Musical Direction: Carl W. Stalling. Merrie Melodies. January 3, 1942.

Sammy Seagull and Cecil Crow become rivals for the seductive Lelani.

CRAZY CRUISE ★★
Story: Michael Maltese; Animation: Rod Scribner; Musical Direction: Carl W. Stalling; Producer: Leon Schlesinger. Merrie Melodies. March 26, 1942.

Spot gags all the way from a Southern tobacco plantation, to Havana, to the Alps, to the Pyramids, to a surprise appearance by Bugs Bunny.

SPEAKING OF ANIMALS series
One reel each, black and white, produced by Paramount Pictures, Inc., 1941–1949. Directors for the series were Lou Lilly and Lew Landers; writers were Walter Anthony, Dave Mitchell, Lou Lilly, and Charles Shows; narrator was Ken Carpenter. Records here are incomplete, but as Avery recalls, he worked on the first three. These were:

SPEAKING OF ANIMALS DOWN ON THE FARM
August 18, 1941.

SPEAKING OF ANIMALS IN A PET SHOP
September 5, 1941.

SPEAKING OF ANIMALS IN THE ZOO
October 31, 1941.

1942–1955: Metro-Goldwyn-Mayer cartoons. Records and credits here are far more accurate and all but unimpeachable. MGM was kind enough to lend us its production records, and dates given here are actual release dates. Credits have been copied from the films where possible, and otherwise taken from existing copyright information. Where no credit but Avery's is listed, no others are known to have been recorded. (The Library of Congress, in fact, made one attempt to go to Avery to gain credit information on some of these films. It was not successful.) Again, I have noted the appearance of any recurring character in each specific cartoon.

1942

THE BLITZ WOLF ★★★
Director: Tex Avery; Story: Rich Hogan; Animation: Ray Abrams, Irven Spence, Preston Blair, Ed Love; Music: Scott Bradley. August 22, 1942. Nominated for the Academy Award, 1942 (the award was finally taken by a very similar Disney film, distinctly inferior in comic invention and cinematic exuberance, DER FUEHRER'S FACE.) As Avery recalls, "They plugged the pants off it." Avery's wolf, who appears in various guises and modifications throughout the MGM films, but who never gets blessed with a name, makes his first appearance here. As a character, he makes an admirable vehicle for a series of gag and animation pyrotechnics, and a much more effective purveyor of Avery's personality than any of the more "lovable" characters.

Sergeant Pork is the wisest of the Three Little Pigs; he's not lulled for a minute into thinking that signing a treaty with The Wolf is going to insure peace.

THE EARLY BIRD DOOD IT ★★★
Director: Tex Avery; Story: Rich Hogan; Animation: Irven Spence,

BLITZ WOLF.

Preston Blair, Ed Love, Ray Abrams; Music: Scott Bradley. August 29, 1942. (Re-released December 2, 1950).

A worm with a bird after him gets a cat interested in pursuing the bird.

1943

RED HOT RIDING HOOD ★★★★ (Droopy; The Wolf)
Director: Tex Avery. March 20, 1943. (Re-released March 8, 1952).

Droopy the police dog foils the Wolf's attempted prison break, popping up at every hideout the Wolf can find anywhere in the world, sometimes even before he gets there.

RED HOT RIDING HOOD ★★★★ (The Wolf)
Director: Tex Avery. May 8, 1943. (Re-released May 2, 1953). Library of Congress Film Collection, No. FAA5702. Raymond Durgnat in *The Crazy Mirror* on Tex Avery: "Fairytales aren't so much burlesqued as transformed into brilliantly curdled tales."

The characters in Little Red Riding Hood just *will* not go through another re-telling of that story, and they demand this updated version.

WHO KILLED WHO? ★★★★★
Director: Tex Avery. June 19, 1943.

There is apparently some mystery here that someone has an interest in solving, but the gags outnumber the clues 10 to 1.

ONE HAM'S FAMILY ★★
Director: Tex Avery; Story: Rich Hogan; Animation: Preston Blair, Ed Love, Ray Abrams; Music: Scott Bradley. August 14, 1943.

A Wolf with roast suckling pig on his mind for Christmas Eve dinner ends up being given to Mrs. Pig the next morning as a fur coat.

WHAT'S BUZZIN' BUZZARD ★★★
Directed by: Tex Avery; Animation: Ed Love, Ray Abrams, Preston Blair; Music: Scott Bradley. November 27, 1943. Library of Congress Film Collection, No. FAA5776.

Two buzzards face a carcass shortage and begin seriously considering the prospect of eating each other.

1944

SCREWBALL SQUIRREL ★★★ (Screwy Squirrel)
Director: Tex Avery; Story: Heck Allen; Animation: Preston Blair, Ed Love, Ray Abrams; Music: Scott Bradley. April 1, 1944. Tex Avery's comment today on Screwy Squirrel is only, "He was never too funny."

Screwy calls the dog on the phone and gets a chase going for the express purpose of having some fun in this cartoon.

BATTY BASEBALL ★★★
Director: Tex Avery; Animation: Ray Abrams, Preston Blair, Ed Love; Music: Scott Bradley. April 22, 1944.

Spot gags on the diamond. The Yankee Doodlers play the Draft Dodgers at W.C. Field.

HAPPY-GO-NUTTY ★★★ (Screwy Squirrel)
Director: Tex Avery; Story: Heck Allen; Animation: Ed Love, Ray Abrams, Preston Blair; Music: Scott Bradley. June 24, 1944.

Screwy escapes from the loony bin, and the dog is dispatched to chase him. The picture ends before it's over, and the characters discuss alternate endings.

BIG HEEL-WATHA ★★★ (Screwy Squirrel)
Director: Tex Avery; Story: Heck Allen; Animation: Ray Abrams, Preston Blair, Ed Love; Music: Scott Bradley. October 21, 1944.

A dumb Indian wants to catch a squirrel to prove he's one of the Braves. Big Chief Rain-in-the-Face gets "Singin' in the Rain" for a theme song.

1945

THE SCREWY TRUANT ★★★ (Screwy Squirrel)
Director: Tex Avery; Story: Heck Allen; Animation: Preston Blair, Ed Love, Ray Abrams; Music: Scott Bradley. January 13, 1945. Library of Congress Film Collection, No. FAA5720.

The dog is a truant officer and there is some pretext or other allowing him to chase the squirrel about as successfully as he did in SCREW-BALL SQUIRREL.

THE SHOOTING OF DAN McGOO ★★★★ (Droopy; The Wolf)
Director: Tex Avery; Story: Heck Allen; Animation: Ed Love, Ray Abrams, Preston Blair; Music: Scott Bradley. Based on "The Shooting of Dan McGrew" published by Barse & Co. from "The Spell of the Yukon and Other Verses" by Robert W. Service. March 3, 1945 (Re-released April 14, 1951). Library of Congress Film Collection, No. FAA5723.

Again a Robert Service comedy, including Avery's most successful MGM ingredients: Droopy, and the horny Wolf.

JERKY TURKEY ★★★
Director: Tex Avery; Animation: Preston Blair, Ed Love, Ray Abrams; Story: Heck Allen; Music: Scott Bradley. April 7, 1945. The Library of Congress Film Collection, No. FAA5533.

A pilgrim goes hunting a Jimmy Durante of a turkey. One of the opening shots displays a series of caricatures of the MGM Animation Staff, standing in line to get cigarettes.

SWING SHIFT CINDERELLA ★★ (The Wolf)
Director: Tex Avery; Story: Heck Allen; Animation: Ray Abrams, Preston Blair, Ed Love; Music: Scott Bradley. August 25, 1945 (Re-released October 3, 1953).

The Wolf gets himself out of the Red Riding Hood rut and into the "brilliantly curdled tale" of Cinderella.

WILD AND WOOLFY ★★★ (Droopy; The Wolf)
Director: Tex Avery; Story: Heck Allen; Animation: Ed Love, Ray Abrams, Preston Blair, Walt Clinton; Music: Scott Bradley. November 3, 1945 (Re-released October 4, 1952).

Droopy, the Wolf, and the Girl in the first of the Droopy Westerns.

1946

LONESOME LENNY ★★★ (Screwy Squirrel)
Director: Tex Avery; Story: Heck Allen; Animation: Ray Abrams, Preston Blair, Walt Clinton, Ed Love; Music: Scott Bradley. March 9, 1946. Avery: "A takeoff on *Of Mice and Men.* We had the big dumb dog."

Lenny is a big dumb dog with the power to crush his dog food bowl in his bare fists while thinking about something else. Screwy Squirrel is sitting in the "Crazy Squirrel" cage at the Pet Shop when he is purchased by Lenny's owners to be his "companion."

THE HICK CHICK ★
Director: Tex Avery; Story: Heck Allen; Animation: Preston Blair, Walt Clinton, Ed Love, Ray Abrams; Music: Scott Bradley; Producer: Fred Quimby. June 15, 1946. Library of Congress Film Collection, No. FAA5500.

The Charles Boyer caricature steals the Katharine Hepburn caricature away from the Red Skelton caricature, promising her more clothes than she ever dreamed of and then putting her to work in a laundry.

NORTHWEST HOUNDED POLICE ★★★ (Droopy; The Wolf)
Director: Tex Avery; Story: Heck Allen; Animation: Walt Clinton, Ed Love, Ray Abrams, Preston Blair; Music: Scott Bradley; Producer: Fred Quimby. August 3, 1946 (Re-released December 19, 1953). Mostly a revamp of the main situation of DUMB-HOUNDED. Avery: "You'd never see the little fellow *get* there, but he'd just *be* there."

HENPECKED HOBOES ★★★ (George and Junior)
Director: Tex Avery; Story: Heck Allen; Animation: Ed Love, Ray Abrams, Preston Blair, Walter Clinton; Music: Scott Bradley. October 26, 1946.

George and Junior attempt to make a dinner out of a barnyard chicken. Characterized by repeated Griffith cutaways to the determined rooster making the long trek from the North Pole to the rescue.

1947

HOUND HUNTERS ★★★★ (George and Junior)
Director: Tex Avery; Story: Heck Allen; Animation: Preston Blair, Walter Clinton, Ed Love, Ray Abrams; Music: Scott Bradley. April 12, 1947.

George and Junior open this one as bums walking along the railroad track, but take a job as dogcatchers and spend the entire picture trying to catch one little scribble of a dog. After failing repeatedly, they revert to their former status as bums, and the dog joins them in a gay march along the railroad tracks again.

RED HOT RANGERS ★★★ (George and Junior)
Director: Tex Avery; Story: Heck Allen; Animation: Ray Abrams,

Preston Blair, Walter Clinton, Ed Love; Music: Scott Bradley; Producer: Fred Quimby. May 3, 1947.

George and Junior's adversary here is a little anthropomorphized flame who threatens the whole forest. Seems to be a glimmer of Smokey-the-Bear sermonizing behind this picture.

UNCLE TOM'S CABAÑA ★★★★

Director: Tex Avery; Story: Heck Allen; Animation: Walter Clinton, Ray Abrams, Preston Blair, Robert Bentley; Music: Scott Bradley; Producer: Fred Quimby. July 19, 1947 (Re-released February 6, 1954). Library of Congress Film Collection, No. FAA5763.

Uncle Tom tells a wild tale to his offspring about Simon Legree's attempts to foreclose on Tom's tiny log cabin, the only segment of the skyscraper-cluttered city he doesn't own. The picture is something of a turning point: Avery discovered, in the context of this Tall Tale, the extent to which wholesale demolition was good for a laugh, as long as it was made clear that death had nothing to do with it.

King of the Jungle blows his top in SLAP HAPPY LION (1947). Original animation drawings.

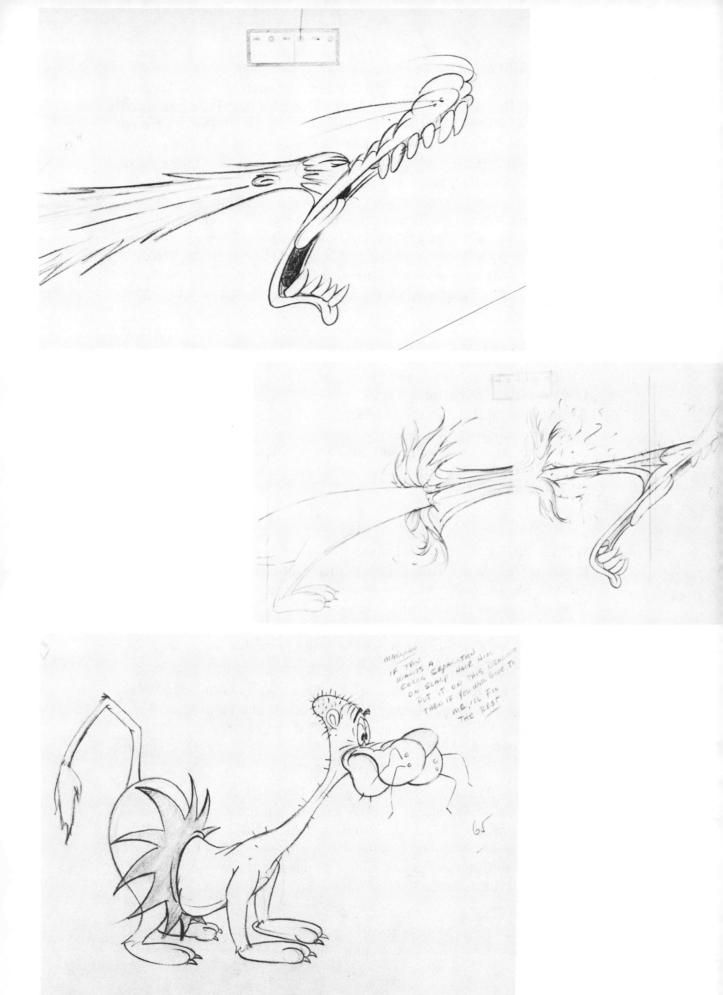

SLAP HAPPY LION   ★★★

Director: Tex Avery; Story: Heck Allen; Animation: Ray Abrams, Robert Bentley, Walter Clinton; Music: Scott Bradley; Producer: Fred Quimby. September 20, 1947 (Re-released May 28, 1955). Raymond Durgnat: ". . . which proves that not even lions should throw their weight about in the jungle, because everyone's neurotic about something. It is given astonishing virulence by Avery's visual ideas. . . . There are incongruities within incongruities. . . . The terrifying and the ludicrous splendidly alternate. . . . People often find this cartoon emotionally upsetting, not because it isn't funny, but because it's vivid too, and they are mesmerized with horror even as they laugh." Though SLAP HAPPY LION has quite a reputation, it's never made much of an impression on me. I quote the above for whatever value it may prove to have to further exploration.

A lion roars his tonsils out to prove he's King of the Beasts, but meets his Waterloo in the form of a mouse.

KING-SIZE CANARY   ★★★★★

Director: Tex Avery; Story: Heck Allen; Animation: Robert Bentley, Walter Clinton, Ray Abrams; Music: Scott Bradley. December 6, 1947 (Re-released October 21, 1955).

A cat, a mouse, a dog, and a canary swallow varying portions of Jumbo-Gro, grow to assorted sizes, and chase each other against a variety of backdrops.

1948

WHAT PRICE FLEADOM   ★★

Director: Tex Avery; Animation: Walter Clinton, Robert Bentley, Gil Turner; Music: Scott Bradley; Producer: Fred Quimby. March 20, 1948 (Re-released December 2, 1955).

Avery's first foray among the fleas, this one about a hobo-looking fellow who forsakes his comfortable spaniel home for wider horizons.

LITTLE 'TINKER   ★★★★

Director: Tex Avery; Animation: William Shull, Grant Simmons, Walter Clinton, Robert Bentley; Music: Scott Bradley; Producer: Fred Quimby. May 15, 1948 (Re-released May 14, 1955).

The attempts of B.O. Skunk to get himself a girl, finally going to such lengths as impersonating Frankie Sinatra.

HALF-PINT PYGMY   ★   (George and Junior)

Director: Tex Avery; Story: Heck Allen; Animation: Grant Simmons, Walter Clinton, Louie Schmitt, William Shull; Music: Scott Bradley. August 7, 1948.

A streamlined George and Junior go chasing the World's Smallest Pygmy, but it turns out he's got an uncle who's even smaller.

LUCKY DUCKY   ★★★★

Director: Tex Avery; Story: Rich Hogan; Animation: Walter Clinton, Preston Blair, Louie Schmitt, Grant Simmons; Music: Scott Bradley;

Producer: Fred Quimby. October 9, 1948 (Re-released January 6, 1956).

What started life as a George and Junior adventure similar to PORKY'S DUCK HUNT develops into what looks like an attempt to make a new star of the little duck, who, if it were not for his annoying laugh, would come off quite well.

THE CAT THAT HATED PEOPLE ★★★★

Director: Tex Avery; Story: Heck Allen; Animation: Walter Clinton, Louie Schmitt, William Shull, Grant Simmons; Music: Scott Bradley. November 20, 1948 (Re-released January 20, 1956).

A cat hates people, so must rocket to the moon. What he meets on the moon outdoes (and pre-dates) the Disney-fied ALICE IN WONDERLAND, so he launches himself back to earth from a golf tee with a nine-iron.

1949

BAD LUCK BLACKIE ★★★★★

Director: Tex Avery; Story: Rich Hogan; Animation: Grant Simmons, Walter Clinton, Preston Blair, Louie Schmitt; Music: Scott Bradley; Producer: Fred Quimby. January 22, 1949 (Re-released November 9, 1956). This is not a Tom and Jerry cartoon, as some sources have erroneously stated.

A small kitten calls on a black cat to dance in the path of the villainous bulldog who is tormenting him. The title card seems to owe something in visual effect to Edgar G. Ulmer's THE BLACK CAT.

SEÑOR DROOPY ★★★★ (Droopy; The Wolf)

Director: Tex Avery; Story: Rich Hogan; Music: Scott Bradley; Animation: Grant Simmons, Walter Clinton, Bob Cannon, Michael Lah, Preston Blair; Producer: Fred Quimby. April 9, 1949 (Re-released December 7, 1956). Library of Congress Film Collection, No. FEA1330.

A bullfight in the Chili Bowl, staged as a contest between the two matadors, Droopy and the Wolf: the winner gets "anything he wants in all Mexico." Droopy wants a live-action Carmen Miranda-style movie star.

THE HOUSE OF TOMORROW ★★★

Director: Tex Avery; Story: Jack Cosgriff, Rich Hogan; Animation: Walter Clinton, Michael Lah, Grant Simmons; Music: Scott Bradley. June 11, 1949 (Re-released March 16, 1956). The original plan for this film was rejected in 1945.

Grand series of spot gags on the home improvements we can expect by 1975.

DOGGONE TIRED ★★★★

Director: Tex Avery; Story: Rich Hogan, Jack Cosgriff; Animation: Bob Cannon, Michael Lah, Grant Simmons, Walter Clinton; Music: Scott Bradley; Producer: Fred Quimby. July 30, 1949 (Re-released April 6, 1956).

The rabbit overhears the hunter tell his Pointer, "You'll never catch that rabbit unless you get a good night's sleep," and sets about keeping him up all night.

WAGS TO RICHES ★★★★ (Droopy; Spike)
Director: Tex Avery; Story: Jack Cosgriff, Rich Hogan; Animation: Michael Lah, Grant Simmons, Walter Clinton, Bob Cannon; Music: Scott Bradley; Producer: Fred Quimby. August 13, 1949.

When the Master dies, Droopy, his loyal dog, is left the entire fortune, much to the annoyance of Spike, his other loyal dog, who instantly plots to make use of the clause bequeathing the estate to him in the event of Droopy's death. Later re-made in Cinemascope as MILLIONAIRE DROOPY.

LITTLE RURAL RIDING HOOD ★★★★★
Director: Tex Avery; Story: Rich Hogan, Jack Cosgriff; Animation: Grant Simmons, Walter Clinton, Bob Cannon, Michael Lah; Music: Scott Bradley; Producer: Fred Quimby. September 17, 1949 (Re-released December 28, 1956).

The Country Wolf is lured away from his hot pursuit of underdeveloped Red Riding Hoods by his City Cousin, who promises better pickings in the nightclubs.

OUTFOXED ★★★ (Droopy)
Director: Tex Avery; Story: Rich Hogan; Animation: Walter Clinton, Bob Cannon, Michael Lah, Grant Simmons; Music: Scott Bradley; Producer: Fred Quimby. November 5, 1949 (Re-released September 5, 1957).

An English fox who reads the Fox News is Droopy's target in his race with four other hunting dogs.

COUNTERFEIT CAT ★★★★ (Spike)
Director: Tex Avery; Story: Rich Hogan, Jack Cosgriff; Animation: Michael Lah, Grant Simmons, Walter Clinton; Music: Scott Bradley; Producer: Fred Quimby. December 24, 1949 (Re-released April 27, 1956).

A cat has his eyes on a household canary, but to get past the household's vicious watchdog he has to masquerade as the dog next door—which he does by ripping the dog's scalp off, wearing it on his own head, and saying, "Bow Wow!"

1950

VENTRILOQUIST CAT ★★★★ (Spike)
Directed by: Tex Avery; Animation: Walter Clinton, Michael Lah, Grant Simmons; Story: Rich Hogan; Music: Scott Bradley; Produced by: Fred Quimby. May 27, 1950.

A cat bamboozles Spike by using a voice-throwing mechanism to make his "Meow"s appear to be coming from trashcans, toasters, and other unlikely locations. Later re-made by Hanna and Barbera as CAT'S MEOW.

THE CUCKOO CLOCK ★★★
Directed by Tex Avery; Animation: Grant Simmons, Walter Clinton, Michael Lah; Story: Rich Hogan; Music: Scott Bradley; Produced by: Fred Quimby. June 10, 1950 (Re-released January 18, 1957).

A beautiful Gothic opening, with a Poe-etic narrator describing the torment in his soul, leads us into a pussycat's efforts to grab the cuckoo out of the cuckoo clock. More cuckoo clock gags, and all of them brand new.

GARDEN GOPHER ★★★ (Spike)
Director: Tex Avery; Story: Rich Hogan; Music: Scott Bradley; Animators: Michael Lah, Grant Simmons, Walter Clinton. September 30, 1950 (Re-released March 22, 1957). Library of Congress Film Collection, No. FEA472.

Spike tries to rid his garden of a gopher.

THE CHUMP CHAMP ★★★ (Droopy; Spike)
Directed by: Tex Avery. November 4, 1950 (Re-released April 26, 1957).

Nice series of Tex Avery blackouts, as Droopy and Spike compete in some kind of Canine Olympic.

THE PEACHY COBBLER ★★★
Directed by: Tex Avery; Animation: Walter Clinton, Michael Lah, Grant Simmons; Story: Rich Hogan; Music: Scott Bradley; Produced by: Fred Quimby. December 9, 1950 (Re-released May 24, 1957).

Gagged-up retelling of the Cobbler and the Elves: no sooner is the basic situation set up than Avery leaps into a series of elves-making-shoes gags.

1951

COCK-A-DOODLE DOG ★★★ (Spike)
Directed by: Tex Avery; Animation: Michael Lah, Grant Simmons, Walter Clinton; Story: Rich Hogan; Music: Scott Bradley; Produced by: Fred Quimby. February 10, 1951 (Re-released February 21, 1958).

Spike makes a series of attempts to keep the rooster from crowing. Enough "Cock-a-Doodle Doo"s to last me a decade.

DARE-DEVIL DROOPY ★★★★ (Droopy; Spike)
Director: Tex Avery; Story: Rich Hogan; Music: Scott Bradley; Animation: Grant Simmons, Walter Clinton, Michael Lah; Producer: Fred Quimby. March 31, 1951 (Re-released March 21, 1958). Library of Congress Film Collection, No. FEA311.

Incredible series of blackout gags, Droopy and Spike competing again, this time for a circus acrobat job.

DROOPY'S GOOD DEED ★★★ (Droopy; Spike)
Directed by: Tex Avery; Animation: Walter Clinton, Michael Lah, Grant Simmons; Story: Rich Hogan; Music: Scott Bradley. May 5, 1951 (Re-released May 2, 1958).

Blackouts, with Droopy and Spike at odds once more, this time in a Scout competition Spike wasn't even invited to.

SYMPHONY IN SLANG ★★★
Directed by: Tex Avery; Animation: Michael Lah, Grant Simmons, Walter Clinton; Story: Rich Hogan; Music: Scott Bradley; Produced by: Fred Quimby. June 16, 1951 (Re-released June 13, 1958). Avery: "Spot-gag deal. Turned out very well." As this is such an archetypical Avery film, it's a pity it isn't funnier than it is.

They are passing out haloes in Heaven, but they can't make any sense out of the hipster whose expressions (". . . born with a silver spoon in my mouth . . . raining cats and dogs . . . fed her a line . . . cat got your tongue . . .") they visualize literally.

CAR OF TOMORROW ★★
Directed by: Tex Avery. September 22, 1951.

Spot gags spotlighting the outlandish accessories on cars of the fifties. Only Avery could exaggerate *those*.

DROOPY'S DOUBLE TROUBLE ★ (Droopy; Spike)
Directed by: Tex Avery; Animation: Michael Lah, Walter Clinton, Grant Simmons; Story: Rich Hogan; Music: Scott Bradley; Produced by: Fred Quimby. November 17, 1951.

Mistaken identity gags, as Spike confuses Droopy with his twin brother, who just happens to pack a powerful wallop.

1952

MAGICAL MAESTRO ★★★
Directed by: Tex Avery; Animation: Grant Simmons, Michael Lah, Walter Clinton; Story: Rich Hogan; Musical direction: Scott Bradley; Produced by: Fred Quimby. February 9, 1952.

A terrific situation—a rejected magician taking vengeance on a stage performer by transforming him into one thing after another in the middle of his performance—is not as well developed as it might be, but there are moments of sheer brilliance. The UPA stylization of the fifties comes off best here.

ONE CAB'S FAMILY ★★★★
Directed by: Tex Avery; Animation: Grant Simmons, Michael Lah, Walter Clinton; Story: Rich Hogan, Roy Williams; Music: Scott Bradley; Produced by: Fred Quimby. May 17, 1952.

Surprisingly good personification story, with the young hotrod who doesn't want to grow up to be a taxicab like his father. The heartstring tugs are uncharacteristic of Avery, but deftly done all the same.

ROCK-A-BYE BEAR ★★★★
Directed by: Tex Avery; Animation: Michael Lah, Walter Clinton, Grant Simmons; Story: Heck Allen, Rich Hogan; Music: Scott Bradley; Produced by: Fred Quimby. July 12, 1952.

Spike's repeated efforts to prevent noises from waking the hibernating bear who's hired him as watchdog, and to fend off the jealous rival who's determined to lose him the job.

There is a gap here, representing eleven months of recuperation from overwork. In this time, Avery's burden was shouldered by Michael Lah, one of his animators, and Dick Lundy, veteran of the Walt Disney and Walter Lantz studios, who directed some Droopys—among them CABALLERO DROOPY.

1953

LITTLE JOHNNY JET ★★★
Director: Tex Avery; Story: Heck Allen; Animation: Walter Clinton, Grant Simmons, Michael Lah, Ray Patterson, Robert Bentley; Music: Scott Bradley; Producer: Fred Quimby. April 18, 1953. Nominated for the Academy Award, 1953. Library of Congress Film Collection, No. FEA758. Though this cartoon has received the above recognition, it is little more than a run-of-the-mill film for Avery, and a rather uninspired rehash of the ONE CAB'S FAMILY situation—serving to point out the random sampling which the Library of Congress Film Collection seems to be, and the complacent "family entertainment" standards by which the Motion Picture Academy judges its cartoons as well as its features.

More personification a la ONE CAB'S FAMILY, without quite the same enthusiasm. Again, the son saves his father in a moment of dire stress.

TV OF TOMORROW ★★★
Director: Tex Avery. Story: Heck Allen; Animation: Michael Lah, Ray Patterson, Robert Bentley, Walter Clinton, Grant Simmons; Music: Scott Bradley; Producer: Fred Quimby. June 6, 1953. Library of Congress Film Collection, No. FEA1447.

A Western being broadcast from Mars climaxes this bizarre succession of crazy TV gags, where everybody is a cartoon except the stock shots on television. Much of the live-action footage features Dave O'Brien from the Pete Smith shorts.

THE THREE LITTLE PUPS ★★★★ (Droopy)
Director: Tex Avery; Story: Heck Allen; Animation: Walter Clinton, Robert Bentley, Grant Simmons, Michael Lah, Ray Patterson; Music: Scott Bradley; Producer: Fred Quimby. December 26, 1953.

What begins as a parody on THE THREE LITTLE PIGS becomes a furious contest between phlegmatic Droopy and a phlegmatic Daws Butler-Huckleberry Hound dogcatcher.

1954

DRAG-A-LONG DROOPY ★★★★★ (Droopy; The Wolf)
Director: Tex Avery; Story: Heck Allen; Animation: Grant Simmons, Michael Lah, Ray Patterson, Robert Bentley, Walter Clinton; Music: Scott Bradley; Producer: Fred Quimby. February 20, 1954.

Droopy is the sheepherder and the Wolf is the cattleman who can't stay on his horse in this funniest of Droopy Westerns. Droopy goes to sleep dreaming of sheep jumping over a fence, and the sheep retaliate by dreaming of Droopys doing likewise.

BILLY BOY   ★★★★
Director: Tex Avery; Story: Heck Allen; Animation: Ray Patterson, Robert Bentley, Walter Clinton, Grant Simmons, Michael Lah; Music: Scott Bradley; Producer: Fred Quimby. May 8, 1954. Avery: "A cute show. That was the goat that finally ended up eating the moon, which would be very appropriate now."

The Huckleberry Hound voice is embodied this time in a farmer, whose attempts to rid his life of a baby goat with an endless appetite get him nowhere.

HOMESTEADER DROOPY   ★★★   (Droopy; The Wolf)
Director: Tex Avery; Story: Heck Allen; Animation: Robert Bentley, Walter Clinton, Grant Simmons, Michael Lah; Music director: Scott Bradley; Producer: Fred Quimby. July 10, 1954.

Droopy stakes out a claim on the wide open spaces, and it's up to his infant son to rescue him from the malevolent Wolf.

FARM OF TOMORROW   ★
Director: Tex Avery; Story: Heck Allen; Animation: Walter Clinton, Grant Simmons, Michael Lah, Robert Bentley; Music: Scott Bradley; Producer: Fred Quimby. September 18, 1954. Library of Congress Film Collection, No. FEA398.

Perhaps the unfunniest cartoon ever made. Seems to have been made anywhere but MGM, written by anybody but Heck Allen, and directed by anybody but Tex Avery.

THE FLEA CIRCUS   ★★★★
Director: Tex Avery; Story: Heck Allen; Animation: Grant Simmons, Michael Lah, Robert Bentley, Walter Clinton; Music: Scott Bradley; Producer: Fred Quimby. November 6, 1954.

Pepito's entire cast of fleas runs away from the circus to join a dog.

DIXIELAND DROOPY   ★★★   (Droopy)
Director: Tex Avery; Story: Heck Allen; Animation: Michael Lah, Grant Simmons, Walter Clinton; Music: Scott Bradley; Producer: Fred Quimby. December 4, 1954.

"The story of John Pettibone, an obscure musician whose strange love of Dixieland music lifted him from the depths of the City Dump to the heights of the Hollywood Bowl." Droopy, as John Pettibone, runs around with a Dixieland band of fleas on his back. "This was a cutey-cutey," says Avery today. "This was almost a Jones."

1955

FIELD AND SCREAM   ★★★
Director: Tex Avery; Story: Heck Allen; Animators: Grant Simmons, Walter Clinton, Michael Lah; Music: Scott Bradley; Producer: Fred Quimby. April 30, 1955. Avery: "Of course, I'm a hunter and fisherman. This was a spot-gag thing, but it turned out very well. This came about after a duck hunt, and we got quite a bit of comment. In fact, *Field and Stream* asked for a print; they wanted to run it at their sales meeting."

Spot gags out in the marshes.

THE FIRST BAD MAN ★★

Director: Tex Avery; Story: Heck Allen; Narrator: Tex Ritter; Animation: Walter Clinton, Ray Patterson, Michael Lah, Grant Simmons; Music: Scott Bradley; Producer: Fred Quimby. September 30, 1955. Library of Congress Film Collection, No. FEA422. Avery's comments on this are interesting: "THE FIRST BAD MAN wasn't bad. The posse and everybody was riding around on dinosaurs."

In One Million B.C., Texas was a continent, and the jail they built for Western civilization's first bad man is standing to this day—and the first bad man is still waiting to be let out.

DEPUTY DROOPY ★★★ (Droopy)

Directors: Tex Avery, Michael Lah; Story: Heck Allen; Animation: Ed Barge, Irven Spence, Kenneth Muse, Lewis Marshall, Walter Clinton, Ray Patterson; Music: Scott Bradley; Producer: Fred Quimby. October 28, 1955.

Droopy has very little to do in what is basically a re-make of ROCK-A-BYE BEAR: two desperadoes, after the stash in the safe, try to avoid waking up the sheriff, and find themselves running off to a distant hill to make the noises Deputy Droopy succeeds in eliciting from them.

CELLBOUND ★★★

Directors: Tex Avery, Michael Lah; Story: Heck Allen; Animation: Kenneth Muse, Ed Barge, Irven Spence, Michael Lah; Music: Scott Bradley. November 25, 1955.

A "life member" of Sing Song prison digs himself a tunnel with a spoon, and makes his escape after twenty years of digging—into the warden's television set, where he must masquerade as all three channels.

While Avery was at MGM, the following projects were abandoned or rejected by management: *The Big Bad Baby Sitter, Chicken Hearted, Dog's Best Friend, Droopy Dog Returns, Droopy's Dog License, Droopy's Serenade, Elephant a la King, Hark Hark the Bark,* and *Holland Story.*

After Avery left the studio, the following cartoons were released with his name on them:

MILLIONAIRE DROOPY

Director: Tex Avery; Story: Jack Cosgriff, Rich Hogan; Animation: Michael Lah, Grant Simmons, Walter Clinton, Bob Cannon; Music: Scott Bradley; Producers: Joseph Barbera, William Hanna. September 21, 1956. Cinemascope re-make of WAGS TO RICHES.

CAT'S MEOW

Director: Tex Avery; Producers: Joseph Barbera, William Hanna; Story: Rich Hogan; Animation: Walter Clinton, Michael Lah, Grant Simmons; Music: Scott Bradley. January 25, 1957. Cinemascope re-make of VENTRILOQUIST CAT. Hanna and Barbera took the animation drawings made for the original, and made new cels and new backgrounds for them. Unfortunately, they've adapted the film to the UPA drawing style that isn't suited to Avery's humor, and they've expanded the normal aspect ratio to a Cinemascope ratio, which is no help either. Shots that looked fine in the original version look pale and unfunny in this.

1954–1955: Walter Lantz Cartoons. These were produced at Walter Lantz Studios in Hollywood and released by Universal-International. Dates given are release dates, and credits are from the films and from existing copyright information. The overlap in years is probably a result of MGM maintaining a greater backlog of cartoons than the Lantz studio.

1954

I'M COLD ★★★★ (Chilly Willy)
Director: Tex Avery; Story: Homer Brightman; Animators: Ray Abrams, Don Patterson, La Verne Harding; Set Design: Raymond Jacobs; Music: Clarence Wheeler; Producer: Walter Lantz. December 20, 1954. The first Chilly Willy cartoon was directed by Paul Smith and released in 1953. Avery modified the character and shortened him, and this is his second cartoon. It was later distributed by Castle Films as SOME LIKE IT NOT.

Chilly Willy tries to keep warm for the winter by swiping a fur from the Watt Fur Co. In this case, the humor comes from the "dumb dog" who is guarding the furs.

1955

CRAZY MIXED-UP PUP ★★★
Written and Directed by: Tex Avery; Animation: La Verne Harding, Don Patterson, Ray Abrams; Set Design: Raymond Jacobs; Music: Clarence Wheeler; Producer: Walter Lantz. February 14, 1955. Nominated for the Academy Award, 1955. Library of Congress Film Collection, No. FEA283.

Sam and his dog are run down in the streets, and in the attempts to revive them dog plasma is confused with human plasma. Dog and human characteristics are then prone to erupt from either one of them with a fairly even lack of consistency.

THE LEGEND OF ROCKABYE POINT ★★★★ (Chilly Willy)
Director: Tex Avery; Story: Michael Maltese; Animation: Ray Abrams, Don Patterson, La Verne Harding; Set Design: Raymond Jacobs; Music: Clarence Wheeler; Producer: Walter Lantz. April 11, 1955. Nominated for the Academy Award, 1955. Library of Congress Film Collection, No. FEA239. Later distributed by Castle Films as THE ROCKABYE LEGEND.

A grizzled old salt tells us one of the legends of the Far North: the "dumb polar bear" who had to deal with Chilly Willy and a taciturn watchdog in his struggles to net himself a boatload of fish.

SH-H-H-H-H ★★★

Director and Writer: Tex Avery; Animation: Ray Abrams, Don Patterson, La Verne Harding; Set Design: Raymond Jacobs; Music: Clarence Wheeler; Producer: Walter Lantz. June 6, 1955.

A meek little piano player, down with a bad case of Trombonosis, is instructed to fly to Switzerland to recuperate at the Hush Hush Lodge, the most silent spot in the universe. Here he has the misfortune to room next to a couple who amuse themselves by playing the trombone and laughing in the middle of the night.

Three Chilly Willy films released after Avery's departure from Lantz's, HOT AND COLD PENGUIN, HOLD THAT ROCK and ROOM AND WRATH, were directed by Alex Lovy and seem to be based on drawing boards left behind by Avery. This has given rise to the notion that Alex Lovy is Tex Avery. This is erroneous.

Avery's work at Cascade in recent years netted him several awards, including International publicity Film Festival Awards in 1957, 1958, and 1959 for Calo Tiger ads, plus a Television Commercials Council Award in 1960.

Avery was awarded the annual Annie Award by ASIFA on November 21, 1974, along with Friz Freleng and Chuck Jones.

Tex Avery spent the last years of his life working for his old friends Bill Hanna and Joe Barbera, chiefly on his own characters, Cavemouse and Kwicky Koala. He passed away on August 26, 1980, at St. Joseph's Hospital in Burbank, California. When these pages first saw print in 1975, he wrote, "This book is the greatest thrill of my life. It brings back so many memories and happy days. It completes my circle."

Not a self-portrait, but a sketch of Tex Avery made by a Lantz compadre in the 1930s.

FURTHER RESEARCH

As far as books are concerned, Schickel's THE DISNEY VERSION and Stephenson's THE ANIMATED FILM have already been spoken for. They are both worth looking into, but so full of factual errors it's pathetic. (THE ANIMATED FILM is an "updated" version of a book called ANIMATION IN THE CINEMA. Certain modifications have been made, but the more glaring errors—such as calling BAD LUCK BLACKIE a Tom and Jerry cartoon—have been allowed to stand.) Bob Thomas' book THE ART OF ANIMATION had every intention of fulfilling the promise of its title, but in the course of its development became a publicity spread for the current Disney picture and might more aptly be named THE ART OF SLEEPING BEAUTY. Raymond Durgnat's THE CRAZY MIRROR, a panoramic history of American Comedy, treats animation (and Tex Avery) with high regard, but it is a bad book by a good writer and without a doubt as shameless a perpetrator of the Sociological Sidestep as one could hope to find. Most of the other books on animation dwell chiefly on production techniques and have little to say about the attributes of real *character* animation, though an Avery alumnus named Preston Blair has shed some light on this topic in a handbook he assembled, entitled simply ANIMATION, and available from Walter T. Foster, Box 1045, Tustin, California 92680. Film histories, anthologies, and reference books rarely deal with animation facts and figures, but when they do it is almost always with the "Myrna Loy Western" brand of accuracy that sends smoke out of my ears. Things have recently taken a turn for the better with Leonard Maltin's THE DISNEY FILMS, from Crown Publishers, and there is every reason to expect the same from John Culhane's THE MAGIC MIRROR, Viking Press, and Leslie Cabarga's THE FLEISCHER STORY, Nostalgia Press—on the bookstands soon if not immediately.

My own work on this topic, if I may admit to some partiality, consists primarily of an article entitled "Suspended Animation," which appeared in Gerald Mast and Marshall Cohen's FILM THEORY AND CRITICISM, and the Oral Histories I conducted for the American Film Institute in 1968: FROM THIS YOU ARE MAKING A LIVING?: an Oral History of Dick Huemer; I'LL NEVER GET HOME: an Oral History of Friz Freleng; and WHERE CAN I GET A GOOD CORNED-BEEF SANDWICH: an Oral History of Dave Fleischer. For reasons that have never been clear to me, the Oral Histories have all been put under lock and key until Doomsday (or the death of George Stevens, Jr., whichever comes first).

Anyone wishing more resources should examine magazine articles, including POSITIF No. 12 (1954), No. 18 (1956), No. 21 (1957), No.'s 54, 55 (1963), No. 58 (1963), and No. 160 (1974). David Rider's column in FILMS AND FILMING discusses American animation in certain issues, including March, 1963; July, 1963; July, 1965; May, 1966. Mike Barrier's magazine FUNNYWORLD is very illuminating in this regard, especially recent issues. Contact Mike Barrier, 226 North St. Asaph St., Alexandria, VA 22314, for information regarding subscriptions or back issues. There has been a spate of late of entire magazine issues devoted to animation; salient among these are ECRAN 73, January 11; PRINT, March/April, 1974; AFI REPORT, Vol. 5 No. 2, Summer 1974; and a special issue of FILM COMMENT, January-February, 1975. Also, a complete list of the Warner Brothers cartoons was printed in the July-August, 1973, issue of FILM FAN MONTHLY (no partiality there, of course.).

(Author's Note: Since this list appeared in 1975, the chief additions to the resource material on animation have included Donald Crafton's BEFORE MICKEY, Leonard Maltin's OF MICE AND MAGIC, Gerald and Danny Peary's THE AMERICAN ANIMATED CARTOON, this author's own THE WALTER LANTZ STORY, and a seemingly endless parade of Disney animation books, of which the most valuable are easily Christopher Finch's THE ART OF WALT DISNEY, and Frank Thomas and Ollie Johnston's DISNEY ANIMATION: THE ILLUSION OF LIFE. At press time, we were still awaiting John Culhane's THE MAGIC MIRROR, and similar animation histories expected from Michael Barrier and Charles Solomon.

The French have not been lax on the subject of Tex Avery, and lately we have seen an issue of FANTASMAGORIE called TEX AVERY: LA FOLIE DU CARTOON and a book by Patrick Brion called TEX AVERY, from Chêne. On the subject of Tex Avery as Surrealist, see Abner Lepetit's "Bilan du Dessin Animé" in L'AGE DU CINÉMA, No. 1, March, 1951; Robert Benayoun's LE DESSIN ANIMÉ APRÈS WALT DISNEY, Jean-Jacques Pauvert, 1961, and its chapter "Tex Avery ou le Cosmos en Perdition"; and Adonis Kyrou's LE SURRÉALISME AU CINÈMA, Le Terrain vague, 1963. Avery's work was featured at the International Surrealist Exhibition in Milan in 1961. See also Jacques Doniol-Valcroze's review of THE SHOOTING OF DAN McGOO, "Un savoureux *western* dessiné," in LA REVUE DU CINÈMA, No. 5, February, 1947, and Louis Seguin's "Tex Avery chez Universal" in BIZARRE magazine, No. 3, December, 1955.)

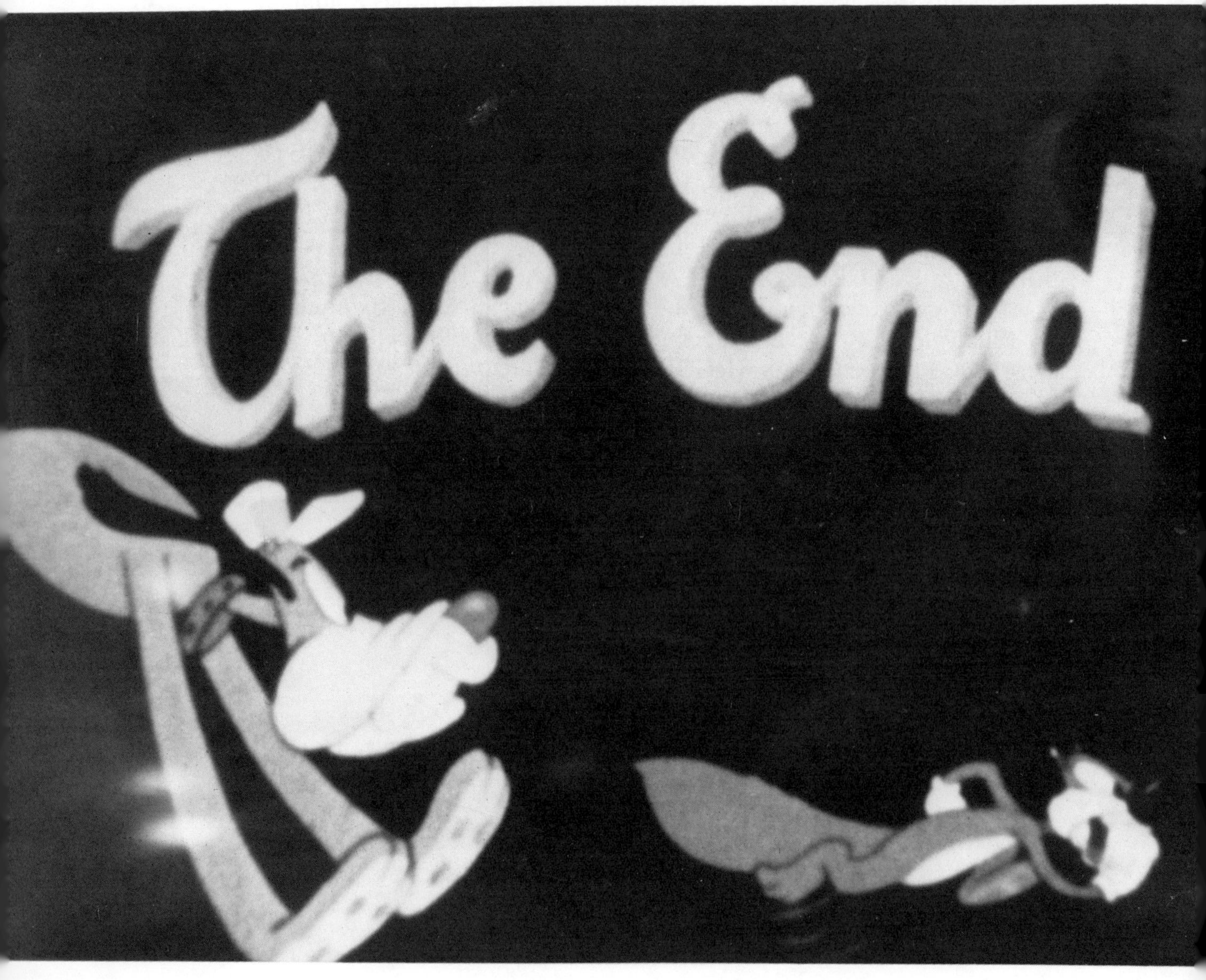
The End

Other DACAPO titles of interest

THE ENCYCLOPEDIA OF
ANIMATED CARTOON SERIES
Jeff Lenburg
192 pp., 180 illus.
80191-4 $14.95

EXPERIMENTAL ANIMATION
Origins of a New Art
Robert Russett and Cecile Starr
224 pp., 300 illus.
80314-3 $14.95

THE FLEISCHER STORY
Revised Edition
Leslie Cabarga
192 pp., over 300 illus.
80313-5 $16.95

FRITZ LANG
Lotte Eisner
420 pp., 162 photos
80271-6 $13.95

GODARD ON GODARD
Critical Writing by
Jean-Luc Godard
Edited by Jean Narboni
and Tom Milne
New foreword by
Annette Michelson
292 pp., photos
80259-7 $10.95

THE GREAT MOVIE STARS
The Golden Years
David Shipman
592 pp., over 100 photos
80247-3 $14.95

A HISTORY OF THE CINEMA
From its Origins to 1970
Eric Rhode
684 pp., 300 photos
80233-3 $13.95

JOHN FORD
Joseph McBride and
Michael Wilmington
234 pp., 104 photos
80016-5 $10.95

MY WONDERFUL WORLD
OF SLAPSTICK
Buster Keaton and Charles Samuels
New introduction by
Dwight Macdonald
282 pp.
80178-7 $9.95

Available at your bookstore

OR ORDER DIRECTLY FROM

DA CAPO PRESS, INC.
233 Spring Street, New York, New York 10013